Access to History

General Editor: Keith Randell

France: Monarchy, Republic and Empire, 1814–70

Keith Randell

Hodder & Stoughton

A MEMBER OF THE HODDER HEADLINE GROUP

The cover illustration shows a detail from a painting of the offer of the crown to Louis Philippe by the Chamber of Deputies in August 1830, (courtesy Photographie Giraudon)

Some other titles in the series:

France in Revolution
Duncan Townson   ISBN 0 340 53494 X
The Concert of Europe: International Relations, 1814–70
John Lowe   ISBN 0 340 53496 6
Rivalry and Accord: International Relations, 1870–1914
John Lowe   ISBN 0 340 51806 5
The Unification of Germany, 1815–90
Andrina Stiles   ISBN 0 340 51810 3
The Unification of Italy, 1815–70
Andrina Stiles   ISBN 0 340 51809 X
Russia 1815–81
Russell Sherman   ISBN 0 340 54789 8
Reaction and Revolutions: Russia 1881–1924
Michael Lynch   ISBN 0 340 53336 6
Stalin and Krushchev: The USSR 1924–64
Michael Lynch   ISBN 0 340 53335 8
France: The Third Republic
Keith Randell   ISBN 0 340 55569 6

Order: Please contact Bookpoint Ltd, 170 Milton Park, Abingdon, Oxon OX14 4TD. Telephone: (44) 01235 400414. Fax: (44) 01235 400454. Lines are open from 9 am - 6 pm Monday to Saturday, with a 24-hour message answering service. Email address: orders@bookpoint.co.uk

British Library Cataloguing in Publication Data
Randell, Keith
  France: monarchy, republic and empire, 1814-70
  —(Access to history).
  1. France-History-19th century
  I.Title   II. Series
  944.06   DD251

ISBN 0–340–51805 7

First published in Access to A-Level History series 1986-Four impressions
This edition first published 1991
Impression number 18   17   16   15   14   13   12   11
Year   2005 2004 2003 2002 2001

Copyright © 1986 Keith Randell

Printed in Great Britain for Hodder & Stoughton Educational, a division of Hodder Headline Plc, 338, Euston Road, London NW1 3BH by The Bath Press, Bath.

Contents

Preface

To the general reader

Although the *Access to History* series has been designed with the needs of students studying the subject at higher examination levels very much in mind, it also has a great deal to offer the general reader. The main body of the text (i.e. ignoring the Study Guides at the ends of chapters) forms a readable and yet stimulating survey of a coherent topic as studied by historians. However, each author's aim has not merely been to provide a clear explanation of what happened in the past (to interest and inform): it has also been assumed that most readers wish to be stimulated into thinking further about the topic and to form opinions of their own about the significance of the events that are described and discussed (to be challenged). Thus, although no prior knowledge of the topic is expected on the reader's part, she or he is treated as an intelligent and thinking person throughout. The author tends to share ideas and possibilities with the reader, rather than passing on numbers of so-called 'historical truths'.

To the student reader

There are many ways in which the series can be used by students studying History at a higher level. It will, therefore, be worthwhile thinking about your own study strategy before you start your work on this book. Obviously, your strategy will vary depending on the aim you have in mind, and the time for study that is available to you.

If, for example, you want to acquire a general overview of the topic in the shortest possible time, the following approach will probably be the most effective:

1. Read Chapter 1 and think about its contents.
2. Read the 'Making notes' section at the end of Chapter 2 and decide whether it is necessary for you to read this chapter.
3. If it is, read the chapter, stopping at each heading or * to note down the main points that have been made.
4. Repeat stage 2 (and stage 3 where appropriate) for all the other chapters.

If, however, your aim is to gain a thorough grasp of the topic, taking however much time is necessary to do so, you may benefit from carrying out the same procedure with each chapter, as follows:

1. Read the chapter as fast as you can, and preferably at one sitting.
2. Study the flow diagram at the end of the chapter, ensuring that you understand the general 'shape' of what you have just read.
3. Read the 'Making notes' section (and the 'Answering essay

questions' section, if there is one) and decide what further work you need to do on the chapter. In particularly important sections of the book, this will involve reading the chapter a second time and stopping at each heading and * to think about (and to write a summary of) what you have just read.

4. Attempt the 'Source-based questions' section. It will sometimes be sufficient to think through your answers, but additional understanding will often be gained by forcing yourself to write them down.

When you have finished the main chapters of the book, study the 'Further Reading' section and decide what additional reading (if any) you will do on the topic.

This book has been designed to help make your studies both enjoyable and successful. If you can think of ways in which this could have been done more effectively, please write to tell me. In the meantime, I hope that you will gain greatly from your study of History.

Keith Randell

CHAPTER 1

Introduction, France: Monarchy, Republic and Empire, 1814–70

Between 1814 and 1870 France changed its system of government many times. The sequence of events was:

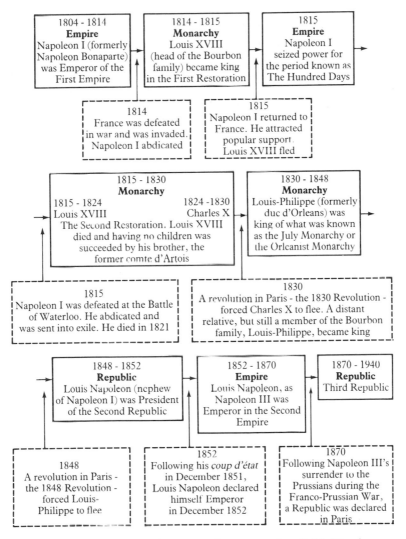

Summary – France: Monarchy, Republic and Empire, 1814–70

During this period no other state in Europe experienced such political turmoil. In none of the other major European Powers – Austria, Russia, Prussia and Britain – were there changes in the system of government until the very end of the period. Why, then, in France was there such an unusual lack of political stability?

The answer centres on the year 1789 when the French Revolution began. This was probably the most important single event in European history between 1715 and 1914, and the history of France in the nineteenth century is only explicable if some of its implications are understood. In the two hundred years before 1789 a powerful monarchy developed in France under Kings of the Bourbon family, whose absolute rule was based on a belief in the divine right of kings. They claimed they were God's representatives on earth, and that they therefore held power by divine right. The long period of political stability provided by the Bourbons was shattered in the years after 1789.

At first the French Revolution seemed to be no more than an attempt by rich landowners and prosperous lawyers to take advantage of the King's lack of money in order to force him to share some of his power in exchange for the right to raise additional taxation. But it was not only the rich who were discontented with the status quo. At all levels of society there was a strong feeling that something must be done to change the social, economic and political systems so as to remove the blatant injustices that existed. Just as the rich objected to the fact that the King's absolute power shut them out from playing a real part in politics, so the urban middle classes, the bourgeoisie, resented a social system in which aristocrats were given preferential treatment in all public appointments and were exempt from most taxation. This was especially strongly felt as all children of aristocrats had aristocratic status which they passed on in turn to all their children. Even more so, the ordinary people, most of whom were peasants living in the countryside, were full of hatred for a system that forced them to exist as landless labourers working for landowners who were legally able to exploit them at every turn. This hatred reached a pitch in 1789 when poor harvests threatened them with considerable hardship and even starvation, while the aristocrats and other landlords continued to live in comparative luxury. This strength of feeling was shared by the working classes in Paris, the only urban area of great size in the country, who were faced by the prospect of their wages being insufficient to cope with the rapidly rising price of food.

In this situation, a revolution that started as an attempt to found a parliamentary political system rapidly developed into an attack on all aspects of privilege, political, social and economic. The King, Louis XVI, who gave way to the initial demands in the hope that he would then be able to rally sufficient support to resist the more extreme demands that were being made of him, found that events were soon outside his control. With no loyal armed forces at his disposal and with the Paris mob able to enforce further changes by violent methods if necessary, he first found himself a prisoner in his own palace and then the victim of a plan to convert the monarchy into a republic. He was executed by guillotine on 21 January 1793, a fate shared by some other members of his family and by numerous aristocrats as the First Republic rapidly earned for itself a reputation for extreme action in pursuit of its goals of 'liberty, equality and fraternity'. Liberty and equality could be worked for inside France, as indeed they were by the destruction of the whole system of political, social and economic privilege and its replacement by a system which recognised all citizens as equal under the law. But fraternity (treating all men as brothers) implied helping those ordinary people abroad who were forced to live out their lives under the tyranny of despotic rulers. The First Republic spent its early years defending its frontiers against the attacks of the European Powers who wished to crush the revolutionary fervour before it could be exported to their territories. Once the dangers were overcome, it found itself invading the Netherlands, Germany and Italy in an attempt to encourage revolutionary activity abroad.

It was expected that the armies of France, made up largely of untrained men and led by officers of little experience, would soon be defeated. Much to everyone's surprise just the opposite happened. The traditional armies of Europe, brought up on a formalized approach to warfare in which it was more important to safeguard men than to win battles, were no match for the mass armies of France which rushed their enemies with little regard for the casualties they sustained. The First Republic, therefore, was not only successful in resisting the attempts to crush it; it was also able to carry its message abroad.

The ordinary people of France were much in favour of what the Revolution had achieved. The peasants, especially, had gained greatly. Not only were they freed from the frequently arbitrary rule of aristocratic landlords, but they were also given an opportunity to acquire their own land by the Government which had confiscated the estates of aristocrats who had either fled or been executed, and of the Church and the monasteries. The bourgeoisie had also benefited. The decision to make appointments to all posts in the Government's service on the basis of merit rather than of birth and influence had resulted in many of them obtaining public office or gaining promotion from the inferior positions they had previously occupied. So many aristocrats had fled or been guillotined that France was now short of well-educated and experienced men to fill senior posts.

Thus there was created a large group of people for whom Republican forms of government were associated with approaches and policies that were much to their liking. As the years went by, and as many of the hardships that had accompanied the Revolution were forgotten, Republicanism became even more identified in the popular mind with a concern for the well-being of the poor, with equality of opportunity, with a time when 'respecting your betters' was no longer a necessity, with excitement and with hope for the future. This general leaning towards republicanism was not restricted to those who had experienced the events of the 1790s. In many homes children grew up in the early decades of the nineteenth century surrounded by stories of how good things used to be in the 'golden age' when France was a republic. So a large section of the French population in the years 1814–1870 felt an emotional, even sentimental, attraction to Republicanism, even if they were not sufficiently strongly motivated to take any action to bring a republic into existence. This of course was the province of the Republican activists who were important but who, at any one time throughout the period, could be numbered in hundreds rather than thousands.

These were mostly people with a burning sense of social justice who were prepared to risk their lives in order to sweep away what they saw as an unequal society. They were to be found at the heart of most of the plots to overthrow the Government that occurred between 1814 and 1870, and were much in evidence during the successful revolutions of 1830 and 1848. They suffered, though, from a lack of organization and of knowledge about the ways of the world, and they often found that others capitalized on the revolutionary fervour they had built up. Yet, although Republican activity was a destabilizing force for most of the period 1814–1870, the main significance of Republicanism was that it was always there, available as an alternative to the present form of government if the current regime was a monarchy or empire and was running into difficulties. If the undercurrent of emotional republicanism had not existed it might have been possible for the regimes in power in 1830, 1848 and 1870 to overcome their difficulties instead of collapsing.

If this had been the whole story France would have become a republic and would have stayed a republic. Why did this not happen? Just as there were large numbers of French people who had Republican sympathies, so there were many for whom Republicanism was anathema. These Anti-Republicans viewed the First Republic as a period of legalized banditry when no life and no property had been safe from attack by the Government of the moment. They had seen one Republican Government replaced by another in rapid succession, each one taking care to execute all its potential enemies. They had seen a breakdown of law and order throughout the country, with nobody able to feel secure about the future. Strangely enough, many of these Anti-Republicans were people who had benefited directly from the work of the Revolution. This was especially true of peasant farmers, many of whom, having gained their land, became very conservative, wishing for no further change. They were particularly suspicious of politicians whom they tended to view as self-seeking troublemakers without whom the country would be a better place. They desired a strong government which would maintain law and order but would leave the people to get on with living their own lives.

The trouble was that the Anti-Republicans were not united. Some favoured a return of the Bourbon Monarchy, for although Louis XVI had been guillotined and his son, who is referred to as Louis XVII although he was never accepted as king, had died in captivity two years later, there were brothers of the ex-King to carry on the royal line. Many of these Legitimists – those who supported the return of the legitimate Kings of France – shared the Bourbons' belief in the divine right of kings. They were therefore unable to compromise over what they felt was the will of God in order to reach an agreement with their fellow Anti-Republicans.

A much smaller number of Anti-Republicans, although they were in favour of a monarchy, were opposed to the return of the Bourbons. They could see that the Bourbons were too closely associated with the *ancien régime* (the social and political structure of pre-revolutionary times) for them to gain widespread support in post-revolutionary France. These people pinned their faith on the duc d'Orléans, a Bourbon himself although a distant relative of Louis XVI and his brothers, because he had shown himself to be prepared to accept most of the changes brought about by the Revolution. These Orleanists, as the supporters of the duc d'Orléans were called, were few in number but were well placed in Paris to have an effect on events.

Perhaps the largest group of Anti-Republicans, at least in terms of general emotional support, were the Bonapartists. Napoleon Bonaparte had emerged from the turmoil of the Revolution as the one man able to win and retain the support of both the army and the politicians. Coming to power first in 1799, he had consolidated his position so rapidly that within five years he had been able to declare himself Emperor. He was a charismatic leader and an outstanding military commander. Under his guidance France built up the largest European Empire there had been for a thousand years, and many were prepared to support him because of the strong government, power and glory he provided. Even after his defeat, exile and death there was widespread sympathy for his cause, especially as there was always a member of his family ready to carry on the Napoleonic tradition. The Bonapartists, however, were not an organized group, and after 1815 lacked support among the new men of power who had risen to prominence during the Emperor's reign, for such people could see that the other European Powers would not be prepared to accept a return of a member of the Bonaparte family to power.

In 1814 France was a politically divided country. It remained so for the following sixty years, such was the depth of suspicion that Republicans, Legitimists, Orleanists and Bonapartists felt for each other. Had the divisions merely been on class lines they might have been less important, for a united propertied class could probably have imposed its will on the nation. But the divisions ran vertically through society, not horizontally. Each class could boast supporters of each group, so there were always leaders and numerous followers content to see the existing regime collapse in the hope that it would be replaced by one that was to their liking. In fact, the supporters of the regime of the moment were often in a minority and were therefore likely to be overwhelmed whenever the

Government entered a period of particular unpopularity. France was politically unstable between 1814 and 1870 because there were so many possible forms of government available, with no one of them able to attract solid majority support for long.

The story of this book is the story of the attempts made to establish a stable regime and of the reasons why each failed in turn.

Making notes on '*Introduction, France: Monarchy, Republic and Empire 1814–70*'

It is hoped that the brief introductory chapter will establish in your mind the general shape of French history during the period 1814 to 1870. To help reinforce this it might be helpful to make two types of notes.

1. A date chart, using the summary on page 1, showing the main periods and significant events. You will find this useful to be able to refer to as you read the rest of the book.
2. A brief answer to the question, 'why was France so politically unstable between 1814 and 1870?'. Your main point will be 'because the country was so politically divided'. Mention the divisions between those who were in favour of what the Revolution did and those who were against it; and between Republicans and Anti-Republicans. Briefly describe the three groups of Anti-Republicans.

Remember that these issues will be dealt with in greater detail in other parts of the book.

Answering essay questions on '*France: Monarchy, Republic and Empire, 1814–1870*'

You might be asked to answer essay questions covering:

either the whole or a large part of the period,
or   one of the limited periods into which the history of France 1814–1870 falls.

You should prepare yourself to answer questions of either type.

In this short section the types of question covering the wider period will be introduced, so that you can have them in mind as you read the rest of the book. They are discussed in greater detail on pages 130–131, which you should study once you have read the whole book.

Discussions of typical questions on the more limited periods are to be found at the end of the chapters 2, 3, 4 and 6.

Questions which cover the wider period tend to concentrate on a single issue: the reasons why France experienced such political instability between 1814 and 1870. Typical questions, relating to either the whole period or at least more than one regime are:

'Why was France unable to find a durable form of government between 1815 and 1871?' (London, 1981)

'Explain the instability of the regimes in France in the period 1815–52.' (AEB, 1981)

'What made French politics unstable between 1815 and 1848?' (Cambridge, 1982)

In questions of this type you are invited to identify the *causes* of the instability. From your reading of the preceding chapter you will already have a good idea of what these were.

You might find it helpful to write down on a piece of paper, which you can use as a book mark for this book, the paragraph headings you already know would be useful in answering questions such as the three above. As you read each of the following chapters, jot down on the book mark any further causes you come across. You might also write a few words to indicate which are the important pieces of evidence you would include in an essay to support the general analytical points you are making.

CHAPTER 2

The Restored Bourbon Monarchy, 1814–1830

1 The Restoration of the Bourbons

In 1810 France dominated most of Europe. From the Mediterranean to the Baltic and from the Atlantic to the Adriatic, states were either under direct French control or ruled by friends and relations of the French Emperor, Napoleon I, or were bound to France by treaties that had been forced on them after military defeat. Never before in modern times had one state been able to establish such a dominant position in European affairs.

It is fascinating to conjecture what might have happened had Napoleon been satisfied with what he had achieved by 1810. It is hard to imagine that he could have been defeated militarily. Russia was the only potentially hostile power which had an army large enough to challenge the French, but it is unlikely that the Tsar Alexander I would have risked an all out attack on the French army in Poland and Germany. The experience of the last ten years had shown that such an attack would probably be fruitless, and certainly the potential gains did not make such a risk worthwhile. Britain, the only other European power to resist Napoleon with any degree of success, could hope to achieve little on her own. Her command of the seas was important to ensure a continuation of colonial trade but it could do little to damage Napoleon. Europe was self-sufficient in essentials and could do without the luxuries which British naval power denied her. The British army, although quite effective by the standards of the day, was pathetically small when compared with the forces at Napoleon's command. It could aspire to being little more than an irritant to the Emperor. Certainly it could not bring about the collapse of his Empire.

So Napoleon had only himself to blame for the disasters which were to overwhelm him. His major error was to attempt to destroy Russia as a military force. In 1812 the might of France, her allies and satellites was marched into Russia where a savage winter wrought havoc among the invading forces, killing and incapacitating so many that it was not difficult for Alexander's armies to finish what the weather had begun. Napoleon retreated from Russia having lost most of his battle-hardened men, and although he was able to raise fresh armies in a remarkably short time, the damage had been done. The myth of his invincibility had been exploded and it was plain to see that with the pick of his armies dead he must be vulnerable to a concerted attack. So once again Russia, Austria, Prussia and Britain allied together in an attempt to restrict Napoleon's power to the boundaries of France.

Yet all was not straightforward for the Allies. In Germany, the major theatre of the war, where Napoleon faced Russia, Austria and Prussia, the French showed that they still had a leader who could outmanoeuvre any opposition and snatch victories from the most unpromising situations. But the victories of 1813 and 1814 could not be decisive for Napoleon, given the position of relative weakness from which he was now operating. In fact, he could not even afford his victories, for it was becoming increasingly difficult to replace the men he lost, in contrast to his enemies who could call on plentiful reserves of both men and materials. Even the British armies were able to taste victory. In Spain, fighting under the Duke of Wellington, they were able to defeat the French-backed regime of Joseph, Napoleon's brother, while the majority of French armies were heavily engaged elsewhere.

Napoleon had great strengths and great weaknesses. One of his most marked weaknesses was his refusal to settle for second best, even when it was all that was on offer. He was therefore unwilling to negotiate a peace with the Allies, even when it was obvious that he had no hope of winning the war. Had he been prepared to accept a contraction of his Empire, it is likely that he would have secured peace on terms that would have left France with much more territory than she had held in 1789 before the Revolutionary and Napoleonic Wars had started. Any possibility of replacing him as the ruler of France would have been out of the question, such was his widely accepted international standing. But this was not to be, and Napoleon fought on against all the odds, deceiving himself that victory lay just around the corner. Eventually the allied armies entered France from both the north-east and the south-west.

* It was then too late. Whereas Britain had previously found little support among the Allies for her policy of insisting on the replacement of Napoleon, she was now able to argue convincingly that there would be no lasting peace while the Emperor ruled in France. The problem was to agree on someone to take his place. He could have been allowed to abdicate in favour of this son, the three-year-old King of Rome, but British policy appeared to be to remove the whole Bonaparte family from power. There was for a time considerable support for the idea of transferring Bernadotte from the Kingdom of Sweden to the Kingdom of France. But as he had been one of Napoleon's generals and had been given a crown as a reward for outstanding service, there remained the suspicion that he might be too closely identified with Napoleon's aspirations to be trusted not to start another round of wars once France had regained her strength.

There were two branches of the Bourbon family, but both of these had very obvious drawbacks. The elder branch was represented by the self-styled Louis XVIII who claimed that he was already King of France, although in exile. He was a brother of the guillotined Louis XVI and many of the Allies thought he was unlikely to be acceptable to the majority of French people, identified as he was with all that the

See Preface for explanation of * symbol.

Revolution of 1789 had been against. The younger branch, represented by Louis–Philippe, duc d'Orléans, was more likely to win acceptance in France for he had been a supporter of the Revolution in its early years. He had never worked with his country's enemies, as had the members of the elder branch of the family, but it was difficult to think of a justification for placing him on the throne of France ahead of those who had a legitimate claim to rule.

Of one thing alone were the Allies certain by early 1814: that France must not be allowed to revert to being a republic. Republicanism was now firmly established in the minds of the rulers of Europe as a system of government designed to spread revolution by undermining the rights of the ruling classes and championing the cause of 'the sovereignty of the people.' It was this idea which had provided much of the stimulus for the Revolutionary Wars of the 1790s, and the Allies were determined that there should be no repeat performance in the future.

As the months passed by and the final defeat of Napoleon drew closer, the Allies could still not agree among themselves as to who should be established as the new ruler of France. At last, abandoning hope of finding a mutually acceptable solution to the problem, it was decided that the French should be left to make up their own minds. But this was only a device to cover over the lack of agreement among the Allies. It should not be seen as being an acceptance of the principles of 'the sovereignty of the people.' There was no intention of consulting 'the people' of France through any system of voting; it was merely hoped that an acceptable leader would 'emerge'.

This decision left the way open to the manipulators and propagandists. The most effective and best placed of these were the Royalists who favoured the return of the elder branch of the Bourbons with their claim to be the legitimate Kings of France. Foremost among these was Talleyrand, once a loyal servant of Napoleon, serving as his foreign minister until 1807, but who had been engaged in secret diplomacy for six years aimed at securing the restoration of the Bourbons. When the Emperor was forced to retreat from Paris by the advancing Allied armies, Talleyrand established himself as head of a hastily arranged provisional government and set about bringing to a successful conclusion his years of scheming. Partly as a result of Talleyrand's efforts the British were already convinced that the Bourbons should be restored, and the Russians were very sympathetic, although they remained to be convinced of its practicality. Certainly they did not wish to see an unpopular regime established in France in case it precipitated another bout of revolutionary activity.

So Talleyrand's major task was to show the Allies that there was widespread support in France for a restoration of the Bourbons. It was a simple matter to ensure that the newspapers of Paris campaigned for the cause as they were largely under the control of Royalist sympathisers. What was more difficult was to arrange the 'spontaneous' display of popular approval that was needed. Luckily, at just the right moment, Wellington, leading British troops from Spain into south-western France, entered Bordeaux to be met by crowds shouting *'Vive le roi!'* and sporting the colours of the Bourbon family. This fortunate coincidence, which Talleyrand played no part in arranging, seems to have convinced the Allies that a restoration stood a realistic chance of success. They agreed in April 1814 that Louis XVIII should return to be King of France.

* The reservations that the Allies had can be readily understood. Louis was fat, 59 years old, and walked with difficulty. His unimpressive appearance was matched by a personality that was dull and uninspiring, and although he possessed a fair degree of intelligence he had shown himself to be a poor judge of both people and events. He was known to be a firm believer in the divine right of kings, and to regard the Revolution as one of history's greatest crimes. He had lived outside France for more than twenty years, surrounded by fellow *émigrés*, all awaiting the time when they could return to claim what they believed was rightfully theirs. It was hard for anyone to imagine that he would really be welcomed back.

The truth, of course, is that he was wanted for what he stood for rather than for what he really was. The majority of the Royalists living in France in 1814 wished for an end to the warfare and economic dislocation that had characterized the previous twenty years. They yearned for the stability and social order they associated with a legitimate monarchy and they gave little or no thought to the details of the person who would fill the office. It was enough to say that he was the rightful King of France and as such deserved the general support of his subjects. But most of these Royalists who had lived in France through the turmoil of the revolutionary and Napoleonic periods were not eager to see a restoration of the *ancien régime* that had existed before 1789. They had not supported the means used to bring about the changes but they had approved of many of the changes themselves, especially those that assured equality before the law, taxation according to wealth without exemption for the social élite, and public office filled by ability rather than according to rank. They did not wish to lose the benefits won during the Revolution; but they did want to gain a sense of security and permanence that had been missing in the recent past.

a) The Charter of 1814

Once the decision had been made that Louis XVIII should be king, the major question was how far he would be prepared to come to terms with the changes that had taken place in France in the 21 years since his brother had been guillotined. To the relief of many, including the allies, he showed himself willing to be reasonable. On one issue alone was he unprepared to move. He would not accept that any limit could be placed on his powers, for as God's representative on earth he could not be bound by rules and regulations. But he was prepared to limit his own powers himself, as an act of graciousness to his subjects. So what could have been an explosive situation was defused and a form of words was found whereby the hard-won rights of the French people could be guaranteed.

The details of the new political, legal and social arrangements were worked out in a few weeks by a small group made up of leading figures from the Napoleonic regime and advisers of Louis XVIII. The King agreed the details, and the Charter incorporating them was published on 4 June 1814. The Charter contained 74 articles and was in many ways a remarkable document, for not only did it confirm almost all of the significant legal and social changes brought about between 1789 and 1814, but it also established a political system that was more liberal than almost any other in existence on mainland Europe. It certainly seems to disprove the oft quoted claim that during their exile the Bourbons learnt nothing and forgot nothing. The terms of the Charter of 1814 represented a realistic coming to terms with the changes that had taken place in France during the previous 25 years, and provided a suitable basis on which the Restoration could have been made to work. For the vast majority of the population the essential articles were those at the beginning of the Charter. These confirmed the major changes which the Revolution had brought about:

1   1. All Frenchmen are equal before the law, whatever their title or rank.
    2. They all contribute, in proportion to their wealth, to the expenses of the State.
5   3. They are all equally eligible for civil and military appointments.
    4. Their individual liberty is equally guaranteed, nobody may be pursued nor arrested except in cases allowed by law, and in the manner it prescribes.
10   5. Each follows his religion with equal freedom, and receives the same protection for his sect.
    6. However, the Roman Catholic religion is the state religion.
    7. Only Roman Catholic clergy and the clergy of other christian denominations receive stipends from the royal treasury.
15   8. Frenchmen have the right to publish and to have printed their opinions as long as they conform to the laws which must check the abuse of this liberty.
    9. All property is inviolable, including what is called national property, and the law does not differentiate between them.
20 10. The state may require property to be given up, for the public good, legally certified, but with prior compensation.
   11. All enquiries into opinions expressed and votes cast up to the Restoration are forbidden. Neither courts nor individuals must pay cognisance to them.

25 12. Conscription is abolished. The method of recruiting to the
armed services is to be laid down by law.

The political arrangements made by the Charter were only of real
interest to the small minority of Frenchmen, known as the *pays légal*,
who expected to play a part in public life whether at a local or national
level. These men were all relatively wealthy and mostly drew their
income from the ownership of land. Some were lawyers, merchants, or
bankers; very few were industrialists for French industry was mainly
made up of small units each employing only a handful of workers. In total
the *pays légal* contained less than half of one per cent of the population.
Yet it is around this small group that the political history of France, at
least until 1848, revolved. It was their support that the Bourbons had to
win and retain if the Restoration was to be successful for they provided
the leadership that the masses were still generally content to follow. Paris
was large and immensely important, but in the rest of France there were
only seven towns with a population of more than 50 000. In the villages at
least, where 75 per cent of the population lived, the opinions of the local
dignitaries were crucial. The political structure laid down by the Charter
was carefully scrutinized by them.

It is clear from the terms of the Charter that although Louis XVIII did
not warm to the political structure existing in England, where he had
been living for the previous seven years, he shared with many of his
countrymen a sneaking regard for the way in which the British system
had allowed the monarch to share his power with the property-owning
classes without this leading to ineffective government or revolution. The
French system established in 1814 borrowed heavily from its British
counterpart. But there were very real differences, as Louis XVIII did not
intend himself to become a prisoner of the politicians in the way that had
happened in England. So, although there was a parliament made up of
two houses, the Chamber of Peers and the Chamber of Deputies, its
powers were severely limited and it was made clear that the ministers
chosen by the King need not necessarily reflect the views of the Chambers. Only the King could initiate legislation and he retained an absolute
veto on any amendments to bills proposed by the Chambers. He could
dissolve parliament when he wished; he nominated members to the
Chamber of Peers; and he controlled all military and civil appointments.
His powers were great, although not unlimited, and it is obvious that he
intended to rule as well as to reign. The Charter turned France into a
constitutional monarchy but stopped short of creating a parliamentary
monarchy such as had developed in Britain. Louis XVIII was in no sense
responsible to the Chambers for his policies or his actions, as long as they
did not contravene the Charter.

* The early months of the Restoration passed more calmly than might
have been expected. Napoleon had exhausted France. More than two
million Frenchmen had died during his wars and heavy taxes had left

everybody feeling poor. There was a widespread sense of relief that at last the struggle was over. The Royalists strongly supported the return of Louis XVIII, but they were in a small minority. For the majority it was very much a case of passive acceptance and a decision to wait and see how things turned out.

As it was, Louis made mistakes, but they were not disastrous. He caused widespread annoyance by changing the flag of France. He replaced the *tricolore* flag, under which the soldiers of the Revolution had marched to victory, with the white flag with blue fleurs-de lis which had become the Bourbon family emblem. He re-introduced elements of the pre-revolutionary court ceremonial which raised suspicions about what was likely to follow. Similarly he reconstituted the Household Guard, made up of several thousand aristocratic officers, which seemed to suggest that it would only be a matter of time before the *émigrés* regained their former power and influence. But he did nothing that was contrary to the Charter and fair-minded people were able to see that although there were winners and losers in the change of regime, nothing had been done to make Napoleon's former supporters feel persecuted. It was therefore somewhat surprising that within ten months of returning to France, Louis XVIII was once again fleeing to the safety of a foreign land and the protection of the armies of Britain and Prussia.

When Napoleon had been forced to abdicate he had been made ruler of the small island of Elba in the Mediterranean Sea, only nine kilometres from the mainland of north-west Italy. He was supposed never to return to his former Empire but his all-consuming ambition drove him on to attempt to regain control of France at least. In March 1815 he landed in the south with a handful of men, and within weeks he was in control of the whole country as the officers and men of the army reverted to their previous loyalty and responded to calls for help from the man who had led them to greatness. It is true that Louis XVIII had caused resentment in the army, especially by the haste with which he had demobilized units and retired officers on half pay in order to save money. But it is likely that whatever the King had done during his first months of power, Napoleon's appeal would have been too great to be resisted. Louis XVIII was powerless and was wise to withdraw to a safe distance.

Napoleon knew that by regaining control of France he had achieved the easy part of his undertaking. He now needed to secure his position against the allied forces of Russia, Austria, Prussia and Britain who were pledged to frustrate any attempt he made to return to power. His only hope was to strike before his enemies were prepared. The British and the Prusians had armies stationed in the Low Countries, in present-day Belgium, but the Russians and Austrians had no major forces readily available in the area, although it would not take them long to bring up their troops ready for action. Napoleon believed that if he could inflict an immediate defeat on the British and Prussians, and then overcome the Russian and Austrian forces once they appeared, he might be allowed to retain his control of France. With impressive speed he assembled his men and marched them towards Brussels. He encountered the British forces near the village of Waterloo and in a desperate encounter, made more dramatic by the knowledge that the Prussians were likely to appear at any moment, he failed to achieve the victory he required. He had no choice but to surrender, and to rely on the charity of his enemies. He was to be given no second chance. He was sent to the remote island of St Helena in the south Atlantic where he was made sufficient of a prisoner to ensure that he did not return to disturb the peace of Europe once again.

b) The Restoration of 1815

The Allies were left with no real alternative but to restore Louis XVIII once more, but they did so with heavy hearts for he was now well and truly identified with the enemies of France. It seemed likely that his regime would be unpopular. When peace had first been made with France in 1814 the conquering powers had been generous, realizing that to impose harsh terms would make the restored monarchy's task more difficult than it need be. The justification for such treatment was that it was Napoleon, not France, who was being punished. It was an attempt to create the impression that an unwilling country had been driven by an unreasonable dictator.

Now that France had rallied again to the former Emperor during his short return to power, known as the Hundred Days, it was clear for all to see that the nation had been a willing accomplice throughout. The second Peace of Paris was therefore much more punitive than the first. In 1814 France had been allowed to keep some of the territorial gains she had made; in 1815 she was restricted to her pre-revolutionary borders and was forced to demolish key frontier fortresses. In 1814 she had retained the booty that Napoleon's armies had gathered during their conquests; in 1815 she was forced to return it. In 1814 there had been no war indemnity to be paid; in 1815 one was demanded, with elements of the occupying forces remaining in France until it was paid. To drive the lesson of defeat home, more than a million allied troops were stationed in the country in the months after Waterloo. Most of them were billeted on French families so that the ordinary people experienced the unpleasantness of defeat in the same way as had the peoples of Europe during the previous twenty years. If the first Peace of Paris could have been regarded as an honourable settlement, the second was clearly a humiliation, and one agreed to by Louis XVIII. The Allies were right to think that it would be difficult for him to re-establish himself.

2 Why did the Bourbons fail?

In the event, the restored Bourbon Monarchy only survived for 15 years before it was overthrown by revolution. It would be tempting to imagine that because it only lasted a short time its collapse was

GREAT BRITAIN

NETHERLANDS

GERMAN
CONFEDERATION

BELGIUM

LUXEMBOURG

Paris

Rhine

FRANCE

SWITZERLAND

SAVOY

PIEDMONT

Nice

SPAIN

Key

Retained by France in the First Treaty of
Paris (1814) but lost in the Second Treaty
of Paris (1815)

Gained by France from Piedmont in 1860

km

0   250

France: territorial changes, 1815–60

predictable. Certainly it could be argued that its task after the second restoration was very difficult indeed. Yet it would be unreasonable to claim that it was doomed to failure from the start. After all, the immediate drawback of association with an unpopular peace was more than balanced by the economic and social potential that France possessed. Much of Europe had suffered dislocation and even devastation at the hands of warring armies while France had escaped very lightly, suffering only temporary difficulties from high taxation. Her land was among the most productive possible and was populated by a skilful peasantry that was more numerous than in any European state except Russia. Her industries were diverse and capable of meeting the needs of the country, even if they were not experiencing an Industrial Revolution like the one taking place in Britain.

What is more, many of the tensions that had led to the Revolution in 1789 had been removed. The peasantry had escaped from their position of subservience as landless serfs supporting a large class of idle aristocrats who were exempt from most of the economic burdens of life. They were now personally free and many of them owned their own land, even if they had to take some work as wage labourers in order fully to support their families. They now had a stake in society and were afraid of losing it. They were more likely to oppose revolutionary activity than to support it. Above them the bourgeoisie, the mainly urban middle class which was especially important in Paris, were no longer prevented from gaining social and political distinction by a system that undervalued anyone who was not of noble birth. During Napoleon's period in power they had filled the vacuum left by the *émigrés* and were keen to retain the gains they had made. They would give strong support to any regime that seemed likely to maintain the status quo.

Pervading most of French life, especially in the countryside, was the Church. The Revolution had stripped it of its huge wealth and most of its political influence which had helped greatly to reduce anti-clerical feelings, although they were still strong among the bourgeoisie. With the peasantry, at least, the Church was in some ways more influential than it had been in the years before 1789, and as a religious revival was already underway which was to affect all classes of society, the Church's role in teaching people to accept the existing social and political order was increasingly significant. Therefore, if the immediate difficulties could be overcome, the Bourbons had every chance of making the revolutionary and Napoleonic periods appear no more than a hiccup in the history of the monarchy in France, just as the Revolution of the 1640s and 1650s had been in England.

* So it would seem that the reasons for the brevity of the Bourbons' tenure of power must be sought in the events of 1815–30 rather than in the situation they found on returning to France for a second time in 1815. Of course, this does not automatically mean that the monarchy was responsible for its own downfall. Quite often governments fall victim to

events that are outside their control, and to a limited extent this was true of the Bourbons. From 1826 onwards France, in common with the rest of western Europe, suffered an economic depression. Many small private banks collapsed, the rich were, or felt they were, under financial pressure and spent less, a lack of demand led to underemployment or unemployment in the towns, and a series of poor harvests led to an increase in the price of food at just the time when the poor were least able to afford it.

In Paris especially, where even in good times there were large numbers of unemployed people who had migrated from the provinces in the hope of finding work and an increased standard of living, a situation had developed by 1830 which was likely to test even a strongly established government. Tens of thousands of able-bodied men had barely enough food to save themselves and their families from starvation. They provided a ready-made reservoir of revolutionary fervour capable of exploitation by any leaders who were influential enough to mobilize them and who were able to take advantage of the disturbances they could cause. This situation was not of the Bourbons' making and given the thinking of the times there was nothing they could have done to prevent it. Yet other countries suffered the same depression and their governments generally survived, even if they had to live through bouts of turmoil and insurrection. The fact that the Bourbons collapsed must therefore suggest that their failure was largely their own responsibility.

a) The Contribution of Louis XVIII

Most historians have drawn a sharp contrast between the two kings of the restored Bourbon monarchy. It is generally said that Louis XVIII managed at least to avoid making major errors in his period of rule from 1815 to 1824. In contrast, it is argued that his younger brother, Charles X, kept the throne for only six years because he committed a series of quite horrendous blunders (see pages 24–31). Broadly speaking, this seems to be an accurate analysis.

Louis XVIII may have lacked the grace and charm to win the loyalty of a people who had largely lost respect for the principle of hereditary monarchy, but he did not squander the advantages he possessed. By supporting capable ministers, especially his favourite, Élie Decazes, he ensured that the Government's finances were soon on a firm footing. With the war indemnity paid off in 1818 and foreign troops withdrawn, the country was able to settle down to a quiet prosperity which was warmly welcomed after the costly glory of the Napoleonic era. In fact it was under Louis XVIII that an effective system for controlling government spending was developed that was to last without major amendment for more than a hundred years. Visitors to France in the early 1820s were quick to notice the air of settled well-being that existed and it seemed that the difficulties of 1814–15 had been fully overcome. Certainly the vast majority of ordinary people were content with a regime that made few demands on them and left them free to exploit the prospect of an ever more properous future.

The allies had been apprehensive about the restoration of Louis XVIII, in part because they feared that a French people grown used to national glory would rapidly tire of a dull monarchy which offered none of the excitement of the Napoleonic era. They need not have worried. It seems that although most French people were pleased to bask in the reflected glory of their country's armies, they did not immediately miss the pleasure when it was no longer available. Apart from the longings of many old soldiers to relive the exploits of yesteryear there was little animosity towards the Bourbons for failing to maintain the tradition of triumphs abroad. If anything there was apathy. Both Louis XVIII and Charles X managed one successful foreign venture but gained little popularity from doing so.

Louis XVIII's armies invaded Spain in 1823 in order to free the King, Ferdinand VII, from the control of the liberal politicians who had forced him to restore a constitution that greatly reduced his power. The French armies were victorious in a matter of weeks, whereas Napoleon, after years of striving, had never completely gained control of Spain. Yet little enthusiasm was shown in France, partly perhaps because the aim of the expedition was to restore a despotic ruler to full power, but also because ordinary people still valued the benefits of peace, not having enjoyed them for long enough to take them for granted.

Charles X's victory was not in the least tainted with the support of despotism. For centuries North African pirates, known as the Barbary Pirates, had taken their toll of shipping near the entrance to the Mediterranean. They had committed barbaric murders and carried off Christians to slavery. Charles X took advantage of disharmony in their ranks to send a large expeditionary force against them in 1830. The venture was a huge success and the pirates' main base, Algiers, was captured with relatively little difficulty. Charles X had succeeded where many before him had failed. He expected great public acclaim as a result of his victory, which he believed would make him secure in the affections of his people. No such thing happened, for hardly had news of the seizure of Algiers arrived in Paris when the King was forced into exile.

So Louis XVIII was fortunate enough to preside over an economic recovery, was responsible for establishing a sound financial structure for the government, and, like Charles X, was able to boast a victory abroad. Yet these were not his major achievements. His great success was managing to convince the *pays légal* that he intended to make the Charter of 1814 a working reality. This he did partly by communicating a genuine belief in it as providing the basis for political life in France in the future, and partly by attempting to restrain those of his supporters who wanted to undermine the Charter, or even to do away with it altogether. These Ultra-Royalists, known as the Ultras, were even more Royalist than the King himself. Not only did they believe unswervingly in the divine right of kings, but they also saw the Charter as a temporary expedient required to win the acceptance of those who had emerged as the ruling class during the revolutionary and Napoleonic periods. They hoped to do away with it as soon as possible, and especially to secure the restoration of the lands confiscated from the Church and the aristocracy in the 1790s, and the destruction of the parliamentary institutions which they considered to be an affront to the dignity of the King.

* Louis XVIII was in sympathy with some of their views, but he recognized their impracticality. Yet, because he did not possess great strength of character, he was unable to resist all their demands. So the Ultras gained some successes. After the Second Restoration 57 leading figures who had deserted the Bourbons and rallied to Napoleon were named for punishment. Many of them were encouraged to escape but those who refused to take the easy way out became martyrs to the Bonapartist cause. Most notable of these was Marshal Ney, a respected and much loved leader of Napoleon's armies, whose death before a firing squad was to give the enemies of the regime a martyr for the future. The Ultras were also able to secure the dismissal of thousands of civil servants and local officials who had been appointed by the previous regime and have them replaced by the friends and relations of powerful royalists. But they were unable to make headway on their major demands. This was despite the fact that they rapidly secured a dominant position in both the Chamber of Peers and the Chamber of Deputies, which they were prepared to use in order to bring the King round to their way of thinking.

In the Chamber of Deputies, especially, the Ultras were often an embarrassment to Louis XVIII. After the elections of 1815, following the second restoration, the Ultras were so dominant that the King called this Chamber of Deputies '*la chambre introuvable*' because he had not imagined it was possible to find such a collection of men who were more Royalist than he was. Here would have been a golden opportunity to carry out a counter-revolution if that was what Louis had wanted. It was a source of disappointment to his friends that he did almost the opposite. In September 1816 the Chamber was dissolved and fresh elections were called using a different electoral system which it was hoped would produce a collection of more moderate Deputies. The ploy was successful, and although the Ultras remained a powerful group, their numbers were not large enough to make it difficult for the King to resist their demands.

However, in 1820 the situation changed when the King's nephew, the duc de Berry was assassinated by a 'madman' as he left the opera. The public outrage was enormous, and was the more bitterly felt by Royalists because this crime removed the only male member of the royal family capable of providing an heir to ensure the succession. The Ultras used this isolated event to create panic among the ruling class and to persuade Louis XVIII that the moderation he had espoused had only encouraged those who hoped for a return to revolutionary activity. The King was too old, too weak, and too tired to resist the pressure that was put on him, especially as the effective leader of the Ultras was his own brother, the comte d'Artois, soon to be king as Charles X.

The electoral system was changed yet again, so as to provide additional Deputies to be chosen only by the richest quarter of the already tiny electorate. In the resulting Chamber of Deputies, dominated by the Ultras, renewed efforts were made to force the King to give the Royalists what they wanted. Slowly his resolve was worn down, and the Ultras gained more and more control of government. In 1822 their parliamentary leader, the comte de Villèle became the chief minister, a position he was to hold until 1827, and the government's policy became increasingly identified with their aspirations. Spain was invaded in support of a despotic King, the Church was given increased powers over the education system, and, most significantly of all, plans were made to compensate the tens of thousands of *émigrés* whose lands had been confiscated during the Revolution. Thus, even before Louis XVIII died in 1824, the country was effectively in the hands of the comte d'Artois and his followers. No great blunders had been made by Louis, but the slide away from moderate policies and towards extreme Royalism had already begun before Charles X officially became king.

b) The Contribution of Charles X

When he ascended the throne Charles must have thought that his dynasty's future was secure. He was well received by the ordinary people in whatever part of France he travelled. The majority of members in both the Chamber of Peers and the Chamber of Deputies were much to his liking, and the succession had been assured by the miraculous – some thought rather too miraculous – birth of a son to the duchesse de Berry some months after the death of her husband. Yet appearances were deceptive. Although Charles was a young 67, full of verve and vitality, and with sufficient grace and charm to win the admiration of many of those who were prepared to respect their 'betters' if they seemed worthy of it, he was deeply distrusted by a majority of the *pays légal*, and it was these people whose support really mattered.

Under the restored Bourbon Monarchy the *pays légal* was essentially the hundred thousand people who at one time or another had the right to vote to elect Deputies to the Chamber. The details of the electoral system were changed in 1815, 1816 and 1820, but common factors throughout were a franchise that was limited to those who paid 300 francs per year in direct taxation, and the necessity of paying 1000 francs per year in direct taxation before one could stand as a candidate. Only the 15 000 richest men in France fell into the latter category. Few of these men had been *émigrés*, and many of them had held positions of power or influence under Napoleon. Their main concern was to ensure the maintenance of law and order for on this their prosperity and their style of living depended. They were prepared to give general support to the monarchy as long as it appeared to be serving their interests, but they could not be relied on to remain silent if they felt that the existing balance of power in the country was likely to be upset. They would rather risk revolution than countenance a return to the royal despotism of the *ancien régime* and all that accompanied it.

The prospect of the comte d'Artois becoming king as Charles X had filled many of them with foreboding for he had made no secret of his close association with the Ultras. Louis XVIII had made an obvious attempt to stay above the detail of party politics; Charles X was clearly deeply involved in it. What might have been acceptable under Louis because his basic good intentions were trusted was likely to be unacceptable under Charles because he was constantly suspected of working to restore the *ancien régime*. So, when Charles X was crowned with all the pomp and ceremony of the *ancien régime*, with its stress on the divine origin of his rights as king, this was widely taken to mean that a counter-revolution was being planned A popular song of the time indicated some of what was feared.

1 At the feet of prelates stitched in gold
    Charles went to his confession.
    They dressed 'im, and kissed 'im, and oiled 'im up,
    Then, to the tunes of sacred hymns,
5 he placed his hand on the Bible.
    His confessor told 'im: "Swear!"
    Rome, the party here concerned,
    Rises anew from an oath thus sworn.

When the law to compensate the *émigrés* and their families was finally passed in 1825 the reaction of the rest of the *pays légal* was hostile in the extreme. The issue was not judged on its merits. If it had been it might have been seen by many as a sensible and fair measure. For ten years the *émigrés* had felt discontented that their loyalty to the royal family and the *ancien regime*, which had led to the loss of their lands and much of their fortune, had received scant reward. Many of them had been given official positions to fill, and their rank and titles had been recognized once again, but most of them still lacked financial security. It was this that they sought, and felt that natural justice suggested they deserved. They would have liked to have their lands restored to them, but even Charles X recognized that to attempt this would be such a basic attack on the revolutionary settlement that it would probably be resisted by force.

So the law of 1825 confirmed the rights of the present owners of the land, thus removing an area of uncertainty that had reduced the market value of any land that had been confiscated during the 1790s, and compensated the *émigrés* by making them an annual grant of money. The money was raised by lowering the interest payable on some portions

The coronation of Charles X in Rheims cathedral, 1824

of the national debt, thus reducing the value of the government bonds concerned which were mainly owned by small investors, the bourgeoisie of Paris. The fact that the bonds in question were paying a higher rate of interest than the financial climate warranted was lost on the members of the *pays légal* who saw themselves being robbed so that worthless aristocrats could be rewarded. Much was made of the seemingly huge sums of money involved – it was greatly exaggerated by being referred to as '*le milliard*' (the thousand million francs). But it was not recognized that the amount received by each *émigré* family fell well short of what had been lost, and was not enough to remove their feeling of being hard done by. Of course, although it was rarely said publicly at the time, it was the principle that was being objected to. Those who had gained by the Revolution wanted the past to be forgotten. They had nothing to gain by the questioning of past decisions and suspected that they had much to lose. Certainly their distrust of Charles X was so great that by the end of 1825 it was already widely supposed that it was only a matter of time before the counter-revolutionary challenge would be made, and would have to be met.

  * Yet it was not a political issue that most seriously undermined Charles X's position. It was the question of religion. It is difficult to realize, living in Britain towards the end of the twentieth century, just how emotional a subject this was in France in the early nineteenth century. Even now, but especially so before the advent of radio and television, much of French social life centres around serious conversation, and religion has been one of the most discussed of all subjects. In the years after 1815 it shared with politics a pre-eminence in the minds of most people and was a truly controversial subject. A significant portion of the revolutionary activity of the 1790s had been inspired by anti-clerical and anti-religious feeling, in its turn sparked off in part by the huge riches and overbearing attitude of organized religion, especially the Catholic Church. During the Revolution and the reign of Napoleon the Church's lands had been confiscated, monasteries and nunneries had been disbanded, priests had become salaried officials of the State, and some churches had been given over to secular use. It had become socially acceptable to be irreligious, and in the towns it had almost become the norm. Among the bourgeoisie, in particular, there was widespread antipathy towards organized religion, and a determination that the forces of religion should not be allowed to regain the dominant position they had occupied in the *ancien régime*. It was against this background of strongly held views that Charles X and the Ultras championed the cause of the Catholic Church.

  Although the vast majority of the rural population had retained its allegiance to Catholicism, in the *pays légal* there tended to be an identification of the Church with the aristocrats, the *émigrés*, and the Ultras. Those who championed the causes of liberty and constitutional government tended to be at best lukewarm supporters of religion and genuinely feared the growing power and influence of the Church. They could see that their views on religion might be used to discriminate against them in appointments to important positions.

The hostility felt towards Charles X over his stance on religion seems to have been generated more by a fear of what he might do than by a dislike of what he actually did. It is true that as the comte d'Artois he had been largely responsible for handing over control of education to the Church in the last years of Louis XVIII's reign, and that his coronation was an open declaration of his acceptance of the pretensions of the Church leaders, but most of the events that caused concern were either fictitious or involved people other than the King and his government. The newspapers read by the anti-clerical section of the *pays légal* contained regular reports aimed at reinforcing the suspicions of those who distrusted Charles X's intentions. The growing number of monasteries and nunneries, which were often illegal but which were tolerated by the authorities, were chronicled in detail. Accounts were given of every case that could be found, and sometimes invented, in which a seeming injustice had been committed by a Church official, especially if the action had been sanctioned or supported by an officer of the State. Most of all, however, rumour after rumour was spread in which it was claimed that the Jesuits were slowly taking over control of the King and his ministers.

There seems to have been vitually no foundation for those allegations but they were widely believed and did much to ensure that suspicion of Charles X's intentions was kept at a high level. What was in fact happening was that the religious revival was gathering pace and was throwing up numbers of aggressively assertive 'missionaries', who, because they enjoyed the general support of the regime, were thought to be its agents. Charles X was a religious man and did see that religious fervour was likely to be supportive of the monarchy, but he had no plan to create a dictatorship served on one hand by the Ultras and on the other by the Church, as was frequently insinuated by his enemies. It is evidence of the degree to which he was distrusted, however, that quite untrue stories gained widespread credence. If he had been firmly established in the public's mind as a King who intended to uphold the Charter, the religious issue might only have been of peripheral importance. As it was, it prepared the way for his blunders to be interpreted in the worst possible light as his short reign approached its climax.

* Just as the suspicion aroused by the regime's attitude towards religion had started during the reign of Louis XVIII, so the Bourbons' treatment of the press had created resentment from the outset. The Charter of 1814 had stated that there would be freedom of the press, although there would be laws passed to check the abuse of this freedom. It had been assumed by most of the *pays légal* that this meant that people would be free to publish what they wanted although they would be liable to legal action after the event if they had printed anything that was contrary to the law. This was not how the Charter was interpreted by

either Louis XVIII or Charles X, both of whom made efforts to prevent the publication of anything they regarded as hostile to the regime. This basic disagreement over what was meant by the freedom of the press made the issue a contentious one throughout the period 1815–1830, especially as a significant proportion of the Chambers' time was spent discussing the many amendments to the laws governing the control of the press that were proposed by the Government at frequent intervals.

This issue, almost more than any other, highlights the fact that under the restored monarchy political life was limited to the few. With half the population illiterate, and with many of the those who could read lacking the interest or the financial security to warrant taking out an annual subscription, which was the only way of buying a newspaper, the daily press reached few more than the 100 000 members of the *pays légal*. In fact, no newspaper had a circulation of more than a few thousand in 1815, and even by 1830 no paper could boast more than 20 000 subscribers. It is true that one copy of a newspaper could reach many readers, especially when bought by a café proprietor or placed in a reading room, but for the vast majority of the population the question of whether newspapers were or were not free to criticize the government was an irrelevancy. But to the people with power and influence in France it was a burning issue, and one which the Government generally handled badly.

Between 1814 and 1822 the Government generally tried to control the press by insisting that no political news or comment was published until it had been passed by the censor. For a brief spell in 1819 and 1820 the experiment of doing away with censorship before publication was tried, but this proved even more unworkable than the existing system, and the murder of the duc de Berry was used as the pretext to abandon it. When, after 1822, the attempt was made to replace censorship with restrictive regulations that would have much the same effect, a situation was created in which the King could only lose. Because it was impossible to frame regulations that had no loopholes, newspaper proprietors were constantly finding ways around the law. In so doing they were placing the authorities in a position where if they took action they risked appearing petty and dictatorial and if they did nothing they seemed ineffectual.

The Government vacillated between a policy of energetic pursuit of lawbreakers and inactivity. This did much to weaken its credibility. Things were only made worse by clumsy attempts at indirect control. At first an attempt was made to buy up opposition newspapers, which was an expensive failure. Then the stamp duty on paper and the cost of sending newspapers through the postal system were increased in an attempt to price them out of business. Lastly pressure was put on the printers of the newspapers by threatening to take action against them, rather than the publishers, if they printed anything that ran contrary to regulations.

The cumulative effect of these policies was to increase the circulation of opposition newspapers, and to further convince many people that

Charles X was unprepared to tolerate even loyal opposition, and was merely awaiting the right opportunity to take away the freedoms guaranteed by the Charter. This impression was not changed in 1828 when Charles, despairing of ever finding an effective system of press control, virtually abandoned censorship of the press. The result was a further growth in the number of hostile statements made in newspapers, and now that the threat of effective legal action was largely removed, they became considerably more vindictive and abusive than they had been in the past. By 1830 the freedom to publish their opinions was seen by the people who were most suspicious of Charles X as their one great safeguard against an over powerful monarch.

  * They did, however, also hope that the parliamentary institutions introduced by the Charter would act as a restraining influence on the King. At the very least the Chamber of Deputies was a forum in which the fears of the *pays légal* could be freely expressed. At best it could put pressure on the King to appoint ministers and to follow policies that were supported by the majority of the propertied class. It was only to be expected though that the new parliamentary system, which, after all, was France's first real attempt to share power between the monarch and the people, would take some time to settle down to effective ways of working. This was especially so as the terms of the Charter of 1814 had established relationships between the King and the Chambers that required time and goodwill to develop into a working partnership. Particularly delicate handling was needed over the appointment of ministers. According to the Charter the monarch was free to choose whichever ministers he wished, irrespective of the views of the Chambers. In practice, a King who selected ministers regardless of the opinions of Parliament was likely to impose almost unbearable strains on the system, and to bring the two partners in the regime, the monarchy and the *pays légal*, into direct confrontation. This was what Charles X contrived to do.

  During the period of the restored monarchy political parties, in the sense in which we understand them today, did not exist. What are described as the parties of the years 1815 to 1830 were no more than loose groupings of like-minded men who tended to vote together in the Chambers and who worked together, if the opportunity arose, at times of elections. Even the names of the parties were not uniformly used and, apart from the Ultras, groupings appeared under a variety of labels. In simple terms, there were three parties in the years after 1814. On the right were the Ultras wishing for a return to the *ancien régime*. In the middle were the Constitutionalists, including the Doctrinaires, who wished to make a success of the system as laid down in the Charter. On the left, although very conservative by modern standards, were the Independents or Liberals who hoped to move slowly towards the British system of parliamentary monarchy, in which the King's role in day-to-day politics was much reduced.

After the somewhat false start with the *Chambre introuvable* in 1815 the system seemed to settle down well under Louis XVIII. The King had his favourite minister in Decazes, but he was not identified closely with any of the political groupings in the Chamber, and was able to win general support from all but the extremes of right and left. The Government appeared to be receptive to the wishes of the Deputies, especially in the way in which the press laws were relaxed in 1819 in response to the demands of the Independents, who, as a result of the annual elections to replace one fifth of the Chamber, now occupied about one third of the seats. Even after 1820 when the assassination of the duc de Berry led to changes in the electoral system which greatly favoured the Ultras, the King's ministers were chosen so as to be able to win majority support in the Chamber.

When Charles X ascended the throne in 1824 he inherited a situation in which the parliamentary system appeared to be developing well. The Ultras were in a large majority in the Chamber, the chief minister, Villèle was one of their leaders, and the King favoured similar policies to those put forward by the majority in each Chamber. Yet all was not well. The reaction to the murder of the duc de Berry had produced a polarization of political opinion, with the Constitutionalists in the centre virtually disappearing as its members moved either to the left or to the right. With the King so closely identified with the forces of the Right, the Independents and Liberals could see that they stood little chance of influencing policy unless the system could be changed to make ministers responsible to Parliament rather than to the King.

An added problem for Charles was that the Ultras were deeply divided among themselves. The major cause of the disunity was Villèle whose overbearing and inflexible attitude gradually alienated more and more of his supporters. This trend had been given a major impetus when Louis XVIII, shortly before he died, had been persuaded by Villèle to dismiss Chateaubriand. This was a real mistake because Chateaubriand was a man of great influence as France's leading man of letters and an expert orator and publicist. He was also intensely proud and ambitious, and deeply resented the way he had been treated. From his seat in the Chamber of Peers and from the pages of the newspapers he controlled or influenced, vicious attacks were made on the Villèle ministry, and even on a political system that allowed an unpopular minister to remain in power. Thus Charles X was faced by a growing political opposition from Left and Right which was uniting around the demand for ministerial responsibility to Parliament.

In 1827 Charles took action to retrieve the situation. Enough new peers were created to ensure majority support from one Chamber, and fresh elections were called in order to win a sympathic majority in the other Chamber. Charles was understandably very surprised when the dissolution of Parliament failed to produce the result he had expected. With the electoral procedure so much in the hands of government officials, it was already well established that elections generally resulted in the return of Deputies who were supportive of the ministry in power at the time. Yet such was the unpopularity of Villèle that in some areas to be associated with him was almost certain to ensure defeat at the polls. Charles was now faced by a Chamber of Deputies in which the government and the Liberal opposition were each supported by roughly 40 per cent of Deputies and in which Ultra opposition had captured the remaining seats. In keeping with what was becoming customary, the King set about finding a replacement for Villèle, so that the ministry could be led by someone who was acceptable to a majority of the Chamber.

* The result was the creation of a ministry that had no leading light and that was clearly intended to be dominated by the personality of the King. So it became more difficult for anyone to speak against the ministry without appearing to be attacking Charles himself, and it began to be realized that to remove the ministers it might be necessary to remove the monarch. But Charles was convinced that it had been the willingness of his brother, Louis XVI, to compromise that had allowed the Revolution of 1789 to gather pace, and he was determined that a firm stand must be made. He was confident that if he remained resolute, right-minded people would rally to his support. So instead of meeting his opponents half way he headed directly for a confrontation by forming a new ministry in August 1829, led by his favourite, Prince Jules de Polignac, who was known to be an extreme Ultra, and totally out of sympathy with the Charter.

This was to prove a blunder of great magnitude. Those who had suspected Charles' good intentions but had been prepared to give him the benefit of the doubt were now certain that the King meant to go against the spirit of the Charter, even if he had done nothing that actually contravened it. What remained of moderate support for the King quickly joined the opposition. It appeared that those who had hinted at Charles' intention to subvert the Charter had been right. The public outcry at the appointment of the new ministry was immense, even though the Chambers were not in session at the time. When the Chambers eventually did meet, early in 1830, it was soon clear that fresh elections would have to be held if the Poligmac ministry was to stand a chance of gaining majority support. Charles made every effort to ensure that the election, held in June and July 1830, was a success. His proclamation to the voters was as direct as it could be.

1   To maintain the Constitutional Charter and the institutions it has founded, has been, and always will be, the object of all my efforts. But to attain this aim, I must exercise freely, and have respected, the sacred rights which are the attributes of my crown. . . . The
5   nature of the government would be altered if culpable attacks weakened my prerogatives. . . . Voters, hurry and go to your

colleges . . . may you all rally around the same flag! It is your King who is asking you to do this; it is your father who is calling upon you. Do your duty and I'll do mine.

Official pressure was exerted on electors wherever possible, but it was not enough. When the results of the election were known it was obvious that Charles' appeal had been decisively rejected, with two opposition Deputies being elected for every one prepared to support the Government. The King felt that it was too late to draw back and decided to do whatever was necessary to ensure a supportive majority in the Chamber of Deputies. It seemed to him that a good way to ensure success for government candidates would be to restrict the franchise to the richest element of the *pays légal* who were likely to favour a strengthening of the King's power. So plans were made to utilize the emergency powers granted to the King in the Charter in order to change the franchise by royal edict, rather than attempting to do so by the normal process of introducing a bill to the Chambers. It was decided to attempt to re-introduce an effective system of press censorship at the same time in order to prevent those who objected to the changes gaining wide publicity for their views.

Having made the preparations in great secrecy, the Government used its official newspaper to publish Four Ordinances on 25 July 1830. The Four Ordinances dissolved the new Chamber of Deputies, which had not yet met; called new elections; removed the right to vote from three-quarters of the electorate; and instructed that no newspaper or pamphlet should be published unless it was authorized by the government. Charles X could claim that he was acting within the terms of the Charter, as he was in a legalistic sense, but his opponents rightly saw it as effectively being a *coup d'état*. He was attempting to reverse the direction in which French political life had been moving since 1814 and was not only signalling that the people would gain no more power at the expense of the King, but was also taking from a large section of the *pays légal* rights which they believed to be inalienably theirs. His reasons for taking this action are summed up by what he said to his ministers.

1 The revolutionary spirit survives in its entirety among the men of the Left. In attacking the ministry it is really royalty that they resent, it is the monarchical system that they want to reverse. Unfortunately, Gentlemen, I have more experience on this point 5 than you, who were not old enough to have seen the Revolution. I remember what happened then: the first retreat that my hapless brother made led to his downfall. . . . They pretend that they are only angry at you, they say to me: "Dismiss your ministers and we will come to an understanding." . . . I will not dismiss you; first of 10 all, Gentlemen, because I have an affection for you all and because I give you my full confidence, but also because, if I gave in to their

demands this time, they would eventually treat us like they treated my brother. . . .

* It is possible to imagine that had Charles X conducted his *coup d'état* effectively he could have been successful, at least for the time being. Most of France was sufficiently lethargic in political matters to passively accept any action by the King which had a claim to legality and which did not directly affect their standard of living or way of life. It was only in Paris that there was a sufficient concentration of economic and political discontent to challenge the Four Ordinances with any hope of success. Had Charles arrested potential leaders of an uprising against him before the Ordinances were published, and brought large numbers of troops into Paris so that key positions, including newspaper offices, could be occupied on the morning of 25 July, the situation would probably have remained under control. As it was, few troops were in evidence in Paris (the pick of the army was in fact still in Algiers), opposition leaders were left at liberty, and the initiative was left to those who wished to make trouble. It was not until 28 and 29 that the barricades went up and rioting took place that was violent enough to persuade Charles X that he must abdicate. While Charles went hunting and his ministers remained largely inactive, the politicians were free to go about their business of planning a revolution.

In the King's defence it must be said that by 1830 the art of preventive action was poorly understood by goverments throughout Europe. By the standards of today Charles committed a huge blunder by attempting a *coup d'état* without taking the necessary precautions. But his stupidity was not so marked if his actions are compared with those of other monarchs who faced revolts and uprisings in the period 1820–30. He can, however, be blamed for seriously overestimating the degree of basic loyalty for the regime.

All the signs of widespread discontent were openly displayed. As early as 1827 it had been necessary to disband the Civil Guard in Paris after the members of this bourgeois citizens' army had shouted offensive slogans while they were being reviewed by the King. The widespread support of the opposition press between 1828 and 1830 was a clear indication of the disillusionment of much of the *pays légal,* and the results of the 1830 election should have left Charles in no doubt as to the weakness of his position. Even foreign commentators in Britain, Austria and Russia were able to see that Charles was heading for more trouble than he would be able to handle.

Once the mistakes had been made and Paris was in uproar, the King's determination rapidly evaporated. He was an old man of 73 and could see that the task of restoring his position demanded more strength than he possessed. He was quick to accept the advice of those closest to him that the only hope of saving the monarchy for his legitimate heirs lay in an immediate abdication in favour of his young grandson, the posthumous

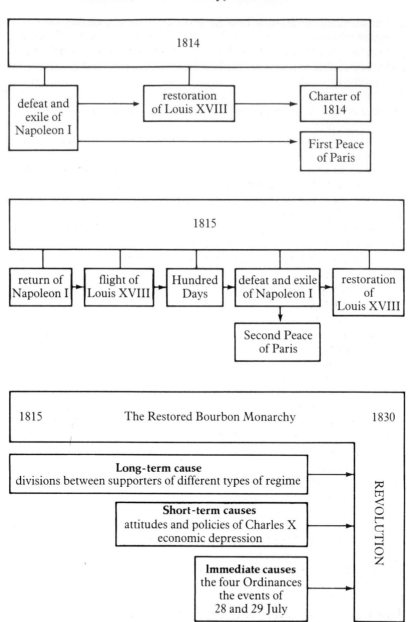

Summary – The Restored Bourbon Monarchy, 1814–30

son of the duc de Berry. This he did on 1 August before he fled to England to avoid arrest by hostile mobs, but it was too late. Those who had seized control of events in Paris had other ideas about who should be king.

Making notes on '*The Restored Bourbon Monarchy, 1814–30*'

The notes you make on the period 1814–30 should help you answer three groups of questions:
1. questions such as 'what was restored in 1814 and 1815, and why?', and 'what was France like in 1815?';
2. questions such as 'what were the strengths and weaknesses of Louis XVIII and Charles X?'; and,
3. questions such as 'what were the causes of the 1830 Revolution?', and, 'what was the relative significance of each cause?'.

The following headings and sub-headings should ensure that you include the main points:
1.   The Restoration of the Bourbons
1.1. Background
1.2. The decision to restore the Bourbons
1.3. Support in France
1.4. The Charter of 1814
1.5. The Hundred Days
1.6. The Restoration of 1815
2.   Why did the Bourbons fail?
2.1. Was it predictable?
2.2. How far was it due to circumstances outside their control?
2.3. The contribution of Louis XVIII
        His achievements
        The Ultras
2.4. The contribution of Charles X
        Links with the Ultras
        Religion
        The press
        Handling of the Chamber of Deputies
        The Four Ordinances
2.5. The events of 28 and 29 July 1830

Answering essay questions on '*The Restored Bourbon Monarchy, 1814–30*'

You will at some stage be expected to use evidence from this chapter in helping to answer general questions on the period 1814–70. A discussion of these questions is given on pages 130–131.

Essay questions which concentrate on the period 1814–1830 tend to centre on *three* aspects of the restored Bourbon monarchy:
1. the causes of the 1830 Revolution;
2. the similarities and differences between Louis XVIII and Charles X;
3. the general state of French politics at the time.

1. Typical 'causes of the 1830 Revolution' questions are:

'Analyse the causes of the French Revolution of 1830.' (AEB, 1982)
' "They learned nothing and forgot nothing." Does this adequately explain the collapse of the restored Bourbon dynasty in France?' (JMB, 1980)
'Why did Charles X manage to retain the throne of France for only six years?' (Oxford, 1982)

Makes a list of the paragraph headings you would use in carrying out the instruction to 'Analyse the causes of the French Revolution of 1830'. In what order would you arrange the paragraphs? Why?

The third question may seem to be about Charles X rather than the 1830 Revolution. But, given a little thought, it can be seen to be about both. So when you decide on paragraph headings for an answer to this question, you will find that they are not very different to those you should have chosen for the first question. Yet the order in which you present your points will be very different. Decide on the order and be prepared to justify it.

2. The most straightforward question on the similarities and differences between Louis XVIII and Charles X would be 'Compare and contrast the reigns of Louis XVIII and Charles X'. Make two lists, one of similarities and one of differences between the reigns. Find a logical way of organizing the points on your lists into groups. You may find it helpful to have two general groups (*Situation* and *Policies*) and to divide these into specific groups. Try to end up with no more than six specific groups. Each group could provide you with one paragraph of your answer. In what order would you present them? Why?

' "Its prospects for survival were good until 1824 but negligible after that date." Would you agree with this assessment of the restored Bourbon monarchy in France?' (Cambridge, 1981)

This question invites you to compare and contrast the two Kings, especially in terms of their degrees of responsibility for the collapse of the regime. Divide the statement quoted into two parts. For each part make two lists of points, under the headings *Agree* and *Disagree*. Once this has been done it should not be difficult to decide on a suitable way to organize an essay plan to answer this question. Which of your paragraphs might be appropriately started with the phrase 'It could be argued that . . .'?

3. Typical questions on the general state of French politics are:

'Why did the Bourbon monarchy fail to attract support within France after 1815?' (SUJB, 1980)
'What factors made for instability in France under the restored Bourbon monarchy?' (Oxford and Cambridge, 1983)

Questions that are, in part, to do with this topic are:

'Explain what was involved in the French restoration of 1815 and why there was revolution in 1830.' (Scottish, 1981)
'Why was the rule of the restored Bourbons in France, 1814–30, so brief?' (Oxford and Cambridge, 1982)

All four questions require answers that make a number of directly relevant points substantiated with appropriate evidence. For instance, the points made in answer to the first question might be: the personalities and characters of the two Kings; the restricted way in which political power was shared; the growing fear of a return to the *ancien régime*; foreign affairs; and policy over religion.

Make a similar list of paragraph points for the other three questions. For one of the questions, list under each paragraph point the supporting evidence you would expect to provide.

Source-based questions on 'The restored Bourbon monarchy, 1814–30'

1 The Charter of 1814
Read carefully the extract from the Charter of 1814 given on page 12 and answer the following questions:
a) Explain the significance of Article 9.
b) Which articles were particularly aimed at preventing the restoration of aristocratic privileges? Explain your answer.
c) The Charter was a compromise between the representatives of Louis XVIII and politicians who valued the achievements of the Revolution. The Charter was largely drawn up by the latter and amended to secure the agreement of the former. Which Articles or parts of Articles were likely to have been added at the request of the Royalists? Explain your answer.
d) Summarize the intentions behind Articles 1. to 12. of the Charter in a short paragraph of about 100 words.

2. The Coronation of Charles X
Read carefully the extract from Béranger's song, 'Crowning Charles the Simple', given on page 22, and study Gérard's painting of 'The Coronation of Charles X' on page 23. Answer the following questions:
a) What is the meaning of 'oiled 'im up', (line 3), in the song?

b) What are the main implications of the coronation as far as Béranger is concerned?
c) Gérard's painting depicts a part of the coronation process in Rheims Cathedral. What are the three main actions taking place?
d) It might be said that Gérard's aim was to glorify the monarchy. What evidence does the painting contain to support this view?
e) In what ways do Béranger and Gérard give conflicting impressions of the coronation?

3 The election of 1830

Read carefully the extract from Charles X's proclamation to the voters in June 1830, given on page 29. Answer the following questions:
a) '... if culpable attacks weakened my prerogative', (line 5). In what way did Charles fear that his prerogative would be weakened?
b) What can be learnt from the extract about Charles' view of monarchy?
c) What are the implications of the last sentence of the extract?

4 The Four Ordinances, July 1830

Read carefully the extract from Charles X's speech to his ministers on his decision to issue the Four Ordinances, given on page 30. Answer the following questions:
a) What does Charles state as his main reason for standing firm at this stage?
b) What does the extract suggest about Charles' relationship with his ministers?
c) In what ways does the extract substantiate the claim that Charles 'learnt nothing and forgot nothing'?

CHAPTER 3

Louis–Philippe, 1830–48

1 The Regime Established

The people who opposed Charles X and caused his downfall were united in their desire to be rid of the King whose style of leadership and whose policies they greatly disliked. But they had reached no agreement on what they wanted to put in his place. The leaders who were most popular with the ordinary people of Paris were keen to establish a republic. They hoped this would ensure a return to the spirit of the 1790s when political power had been taken from those of wealth and aristocratic birth and given to those who could win the support of the common people. The many rich bankers, traders, and professional men who had welcomed the overthrow of Charles X, however, were terrified at the prospect of a revolutionary republic which might not respect the rights of property and which might be in the control of the 'ignorant masses'. They had opposed Charles X because they were unprepared to accept a growth in the power of the King, not because they believed in principles such as democracy. Therefore, once they had become aware of the very real danger that the campaign to unseat Charles X might develop into a full-scale revolution, they rapidly showed their willingness to support a system of government which they hoped would protect them from the excesses of republicanism.

Luckily for them there was a ready-made compromise solution to the problem of what to do once Charles X had abdicated. There was also a small but well organized group of men who took immediate action to ensure that the compromise solution was brought to everyone's notice in Paris. As soon as it was clear that Charles would go, placards appeared championing the cause of Louis–Philippe, duc d'Orléans, as the next king. At the same time many important and influential people were approached individually to canvass support for what appeared to be the only realistic way of preventing the situation getting out of hand. It was obvious that popular support could not be gained for the solution that Charles X had wanted – a regency until his nine-year-old grandson came of age – and so widespread support for Louis–Philippe as the least of all evils rapidly developed among the property owners. Within a few days of Charles' abdication Louis-Philippe became the new king at the invitation of the men who were sufficiently alert and knowledgeable about the ways of the world to seize temporary control of events in Paris as a self-styled Provisional Government.

Louis–Philippe was in fact a very obvious choice. He was the head of the richest and socially most important family in France, being the direct descendant of the brother of France's most famous King, Louis XIV, and the next in line to the throne after the family of Charles X. As such it was only natural to turn to him once it was decided that anybody directly linked to Charles was unacceptable.

At the same time it was possible to portray Louis–Philippe in a favourable light to those who yearned for a return of the dramatic times of the Revolution. Louis–Philippe's father had supported the Revolution from the beginning and had willingly given up his titles to take on the family name of Égalité, thus espousing the cause – equality – which many of the revolutionaries most favoured. He had supported the execution of the King, Louis XVI, in 1793, showing even more clearly that he was in favour of the new order of things. Even the young Louis–Philippe, who had been a teenager when the Revolution started in 1789, had energetically championed the cause. His supporters in 1830 drew attention to the fact that he had played a significant part as a military commander in the successes of the revolutionary armies in the battles of Valmy and Jemappes in 1792. It was true that in 1793 Louis–Philippe had fled from France in order to escape the excesses of the later part of the Revolution. But at least he had refused to support the enemies of revolutionary France, unlike many of the émigrés who had subsequently returned with Louis XVIII and Charles and who had held office under them. Thus, although Louis–Philippe would not have been the choice of the Republicans, he was acceptable to many of the more moderate of them.

* What was this man like who had somewhat fortuitously become King of France at the age of 56? Luckily there was much about him that made him likely to be a successful King. He had sufficient intelligence to be able to think his way through many of the complex issues with which he was faced. He was therefore not at the mercy of the skilled courtier or politician who might otherwise have been able to manipulate him at will. He was hard working and energetic which made it possible for him to keep very much in touch with what was happening and to make decisions based on the best factual evidence that was available. He was good with people, having the happy knack of making others feel that they were important, and thus usually winning from them some degree of personal loyalty. This was particularly marked in his treatment of the large numbers of people from all over France who were day-to-day received by him in his palace, and who went away feeling that they were people of some significance having been treated by the King in such a complimentary manner.

Perhaps what made it most likely that Louis–Philippe would be a success, however, was the determined and serious-minded way in which he set about performing the task which fate had set him. He did not regard becoming king as the climax to his life, but rather saw it as the beginning of his real life's work. This is not surprising because he had not been brought up to be the pompous, arrogant, and immoral wastrel that many of his fellow aristocrats were. His father had insisted that he be given a strict but enlightened education formulated so as to ensure the development of a fine character and high personal standards. Although the form which this education took was unlike that of a nineteenth century British public school, the results were very similar. The education he received, largely at the hands of an aristocratic governess, was to have a profound effect on the whole of his life. A report written to his parents about him by his governess when he was sixteen said,

1 'He has none of the frivolity of his age; he sincerely disdains the puerilities which so many young men pursue – such as fashions, trinkets, trifles of all kinds and the rage for novelties. He has no passion for money; he is disinterested, despises notoriety, and is
5 consequently truly noble; lastly he has an excellent heart which joined to reflection is capable of producing all other good qualities'.

The man of 56 was not the boy of 16 but many of the early qualities remained, even if the events of his life had developed some less desirable tendencies as well.

He spent the years between 1793 and 1815 as a refugee, initially in Switzerland and the USA, but latterly in England. For much of the time he was much poorer than somebody of his social standing should have been, and he disliked having to rely on the handouts from friends and from somewhat parsimonious governments. It was not at all surprising, then, that he displayed some of the traits of one who had experienced being rejected and had known insecurity.

Those who knew him well as King described his very obvious desire to be liked by everybody with whom he came into contact. This resulted in an attempt to be all things to all people, and to say the things that were likely to please. People who were delighted to find that the King agreed with their point of view were less enamoured to hear from somebody else that he said just the opposite to them. It gave the impression that Louis-Philippe was not someone to be trusted.

Springing from the same sense of insecurity he developed an increasing unwillingness to make decisions. It was not that he did not know his own mind, but that while the decision remained unmade all the options remained open and no positive offence was given. This state of almost chronic indecision became more and more marked as Louis-Philippe progressed through his late sixties into his early seventies. To be led by an old man who was all 'maybe' and rarely 'yes' or 'no' was acceptable to those who wanted to see as little change as possible, but it was deeply frustrating to ambitious and energetic younger men who still had their mark to make. This mixture of strengths and weaknesses in the character of Louis–Philippe was highlighted in a pen portrait of the King written in 1850 by one his former opponents in the Legislative Assembly. It reads:

1 He was human without being sentimental, greedy and soft. He had no flaming passions, no ruinous weaknesses, no striking vices, and only one kingly virtue: courage. He was extremely polite, but without choice or greatness, a politeness of a merchant rather than

5 of a Prince. He hardly appreciated literature or art, but he passionately loved industry. His memory was prodigious and capable of keeping the minutest detail. His conversation was prolix, diffuse, original and trivial, anecdotal, full of small facts, of salt and meaning; it gave all satisfaction which one may find in intellectual
10 pleasures when delicacy and elevation are absent. His mind was distinguished, but withdrawn and embarrassed for his soul was neither high nor profound. He was enlightened, subtle, flexible; as he was only open to that which was useful, he was full of profound disdain for the truth, and he did so little believe in virtue that his
15 sight was darkened. Thus he did not see the beauty which truth and decency show, he did not even understand any more their usefulness which they so often have. He had a profound knowledge of human beings, but he knew them only through their vices.

* Louis–Philippe did not become king on the same basis as Louis XVIII had been 'restored'. To do so would have been unacceptable to the many opponents of the restored monarchy of Louis and Charles, and may not even have been to the liking of Louis–Philippe himself. Just as many French people looked back to the history of the Revolution of 1789 for their inspiration, so the supporters of Louis–Philippe had in mind the 'Glorious Revolution' that had taken place in England a century earlier. In this the arrogant and overbearing James II had been replaced by the closely related William of Orange who was prepared to accept his crown from the hands of the people, rather than insisting that it came to him by divine right. The differences between the new Orleanist Monarchy and the now deposed Bourbon Monarchy were therefore greatly stressed in 1830.

The placards which appeared on the walls of Paris on the night of 29–30 July 1830 when an effort was being made to whip up support for Louis–Philippe, the then duc d'Orléans, read (in translation) as follows:

1 Charles X can never return to Paris. He has caused the blood of the people to be shed.
A Republic would expose us to terrible divisions; it would embroil us with Europe.
5 The duc d'Orléans is a prince devoted to the cause of the Revolution.
The duc d'Orléans has never fought against us.
The duc d'Orléans was at Jemappes.
The duc d'Orléans bore the *tricolore* flag under fire; the duc
10 d'Orléans alone can bear it again; we will have no other flag.
The duc d'Orléans has declared himself; he accepts the Charter as we have always wished and understood it.
It will be from the people of France that he will hold his crown.

The last two statements were not just image building as was much of the rest of the placard; they were intended to represent ways in which the new regime would differ profoundly from the old.

In politics symbols are often seen to be just as important as reality. The complex nature of reality is usually far too bemusing for anybody but the expert or the highly intellectual to grasp properly; the simplicity of a symbolic action or stance makes them understandable by all. Several of the ways in which Louis-Philippe's Orleanist regime differed from the restored Bourbon Monarchy were of greater symbolic significance than practical importance.

The flag of France before the Revolution in 1789 had been the fleur-de-lis, the personal coat of arms of the Bourbon family. During the Revolution this had been replaced by the famous *tricolore* with its red, white and blue vertical bands, which had come to be seen as symbolic of all that the Revolution and Napoleonic Empire had achieved. When Napoleon was exiled in 1815 the *tricolore* had been banished with him. Louis XVIII returned with the old flag and many of the old ways of doing things. The fact that Louis–Philippe was prepared to accept the flag of the Revolution marked him out to the people of France as a king who had no desire to return to the days of the *ancien régime*.

The last line of the placard implied another change. Previous Kings had been King of France (*roi de France*), a title which suggested a proprietorial right to the land they ruled. Louis–Philippe was crowned King of the French (*roi des Français*), a title that was intended to draw attention to the fact that he ruled over the people of France because they had asked him to do so, and on terms that had been agreed between them.

There were, however, changes that did alter the reality of French political life. Most noticeable to the historian is the way in which the censorship laws were changed so that newspaper proprietors could print almost what they liked and only run the risk of legal action after the event. As it turned out, the range of legal action available was so restricted and so difficult to implement that Louis-Philippe's reign saw some of the most subversive newspapers that have ever been allowed to exist. The opposition press, making a habit of gross misrepresentation and blatant lying, helped to create an atmosphere in which it was difficult to retain faith in the regime even when it was doing well. In later years, after he had been forced to abdicate, Louis–Philippe summed up the situation well, 'During my reign I was the victim of . . . the printed lie, a cowardly and treacherous weapon which strikes often without our knowing where the blow comes from, a weapon which inflicts wounds that never heal, because they are poisoned.'

The relaxation of censorship was probably unavoidable given the amount of discontent that had been provoked by the efforts of Charles X to control the press. In a similar way, the manner in which the power and influence of the Catholic Church had grown since 1824 and the bitter resentment this had caused meant that the disestablishment of the Church was a clear necessity. Thus Catholicism lost its privileged position as the state religion. Whereas Charles X had made no secret of the fact that he favoured the influence of the Church, Louis–Philippe went out of his way to prove his neutrality in such matters. Leading churchmen were no longer to play a part in controlling the education system, and the income of bishops was significantly reduced. The Jesuits, who had been thought to exercise great influence over Charles X, were subsequently forced to leave France.

The political significance of a change of regime in nineteeth-century Europe is often assessed by the effect it had on the movement towards or away from democracy. In 1830, of course, it was only the extremists who thought in terms of 'one man, one vote', and only the visionaries who even contemplated granting political rights to women. Most of the forward thinkers still assumed that only men who owned a substantial amount of property should be entitled to play a part in the political process. It seemed obvious to nearly everyone that to give power to the poor was almost certain to lead to the rich being robbed to provide for those who possessed little or nothing. As a result, most disagreement was about how power should be distributed within the property-owning classes.

The changes brought about following the new regime in 1830 may not, therefore, seem very dramatic. Only a small minority of men were allowed to vote in elections for the Assembly (the equivalent of the House of Commons) and the system was so arranged that those who could vote were likely to be very much under the influence of government officials or the social élite of the district. In fact the voting qualification was amended so that only men who paid 200 francs in direct taxation were allowed to vote, as opposed to only those who paid 300 francs as had been the regulation previously. However, the change still left many of the urban middle class men without the vote for, although the effect of the change was to increase the electorate from 94 000 to 166 000, direct taxes were mostly paid on income from the ownership of land rather than from trade, industry, or the professions. Clearly, those who had taken control of events in July 1830 had no intention of letting effective power slip from their grasp.

Other changes in the 'system' represented modest attempts to move away from the over-restrictive nature of the regime of Louis XVIII and Charles X. The age at which a person could be elected to the Assembly was reduced from 40 to 30; more locally elected councils were established, but with the mayor appointed by the Government, and units of the National Guard were allowed to elect their own officers. But the fact remained that more than 97 per cent of men over the age of 21 played no part in the official political life of the nation.

With so few changes in the system and with so many of the politicians of the old regime re-emerging for service under Louis–Philippe, it would be possible to imagine that nothing had really changed. This would be untrue. The people at the time noticed the difference. A large majority of the government officials, diplomats, and generals were removed from office and replaced by men who were thought to be more sympathetic to the new order of things. More significant, it was clear for all to see that power was now firmly in the hands of the *haute bourgeoisie*, the upper-middle classes, who had brought Louis–Philippe to the throne, and whose continued support was essential if he was to remain there. The nobility, which had been so prominent during the Bourbon Restoration, played relatively little part in politics and probably became less important in both the army and the Church. Even though many nobles remained influential in their own localities, they had lost their pre-eminence as a group.

2 The Regime Consolidated

To begin with it was by no means certain that the new regime would last more than a matter of months. The Orleanists had seized the initiative in Paris by arranging for Louis–Philippe to be crowned king, and many of the well-to-do, seeing the new monarchy as the only practical alternative to social revolution, had given their support. But there were many ardent Republicans who were unwilling to allow themselves to be outmanoeuvred without resistance. For a time these Republicans were helped to maintain spirited opposition to the regime by the continuation of the economic depression which had started in 1826 and was not to be replaced by increasing prosperity until the mid 1830s. With work hard to find and with wages being decreased rather than increased, there was ample opportunity for the Republican leaders among the poorer classes to stir up sufficient hatred of the rich and powerful to make regular outbreaks of mob violence a probability.

There is no way of knowing for certain, but it seems likely that had it not been for the way in which Louis–Philippe conducted himself the Republicans would have been successful in their attempts to overthrow the regime. The major defence against civil unrest was the National Guard, mainly made up of the property-owning middle-classes. Without positive leadership and constant boosts to their morale, these untrained defenders of law and order might well have come to the conclusion that their interests lay in siding with the malcontents and hoping to play a major part in any new republic that might be established. Louis–Philippe worked hard to stop this happening. It seems that some part of almost every day in the first years of his reign was spent reviewing detachments of the National Guard which had come to Paris expressly for that purpose. Louis–Philippe showed such *bonhomie* on these occasions and was so careful to stress how much he personally valued the support of such men, that he built up a large amount of real loyalty among the middle-classes and created a real sense of unity of purpose.

This feeling was heightened by the personal bravery shown by Louis–Philippe in times of crisis. Whenever there was serious trouble on the streets he was to be found among the National Guard exhorting and encouraging, showing that he was not expecting others to take risks which he was not prepared for himself. The security measures taken to ensure his safety during public appearances were rudimentary in the extreme. Any assassin who was prepared to risk subsequent arrest was assured a reasonable chance of success. There were at least six nearly successful attempts on Louis–Philippe's life during the early years of his reign, as individuals or small groups of republicans attempted to rid their country of the man who symbolized for them the way they had been tricked in 1830. That Louis–Philippe remained virtually unharmed while those around him were killed or injured seemed to confirm to those of moderate opinion that he was indeed meant to be king. His first action after each attempted assassination was to let it be seen that he was alive and well, thus immediately risking a second attempt on his life. This convinced all but the extremists that here was a very courageous man who was putting himself in jeopardy in ways which they would not care to imitate.

Louis–Philippe also showed good sense in his handling of the details of day-to-day political life during the early years of his reign. Although he genuinely admired the style of constitutional monarchy which he had observed at first hand during his exile in England, he had no desire to be shut out from the detailed management of affairs which he realized was where real political power lay. He meant to rule as well as to reign. Yet he understood that given the recent experience of Charles X's attempted *coup d'état* he might have to bide his time and wait for an appropriate moment at which to assert himself. So ministries he did not particularly like, but which were the only ones that could command a majority in the Assembly, were tolerated.

His patience was rewarded. As the economic state of the country recovered and the standard of living of almost everybody improved sufficiently to stimulate hope in the future, support for the regime became widespread and it was generally accepted that the Orleanist Monarchy had come to stay. At the same time the leading politicians had shown themselves to be more interested in squabbling among themselves in a contest to hold ministerial office than in forming a united front to maintain the regime and to keep the King in what they saw to be his place. Little by little, Louis–Philippe took over more control of events until from 1840 to 1848, with Guizot as his leading minister, he shared the detailed control of events with his ministers. Guizot was the one politician with whom Louis–Philippe felt really at ease. The two men shared a common view on what should be the extent of the monarch's power and neither could see any fault in the political system as established in 1830. The King was in many ways fortunate to have the loyal support of a man who had featured prominently in the opposition to

Charles X and who was recognized as having one of the best brains in France. Guizot and Louis–Philippe became inseparable and forged an effective partnership in which each was prepared to share power with the other. Thus Louis–Philippe was a constitutional monarch in that he was bound by the Charter that he had accepted when he became King, but he was a constitutional monarch who was, as he was reported to have said, 'the director of everything and the master of nothing.' His influence was all-pervading even if it was his ministers who technically made most of the decisions.

3 The Fall of the Regime

a) Long-term Causes

Yet in February 1848 Louis–Philippe was forced to abdicate. Why then did a monarchy that had overcome its early difficulties so successfully and which had established itself in the minds of most French people as an acceptable form of government collapse so suddenly and unexpectedly?

It could be argued that the fall was inevitable. Certainly there was a fundamental weakness in the nature of the regime, and it is probable that this would have become more and more obvious as time went on whatever Louis–Philippe and his ministers had or had not done. The restored Bourbon Monarchy of Louis XVIII and Charles X could claim to be the rightful government of France in 1815. Until the interlude of the Revolution and the Napoleonic Empire, there had been centuries of Bourbon rule, with eldest male heir following eldest male heir to the throne in strict succession, based it was claimed on the will of God. Non-one could maintain that the Bourbons did not have a strong right to be there.

With Louis–Philippe it was different. It was true that he had been next in line of succession after Charles X and his grandson, but there was no belief and no tradition that the legitimate monarch should be replaced by one of his relatives when he became unpopular. Certainly it was not claimed that Louis-Philippe was king by divine right. On what basis, then, was he the King? The only bases for a regime seemed to be hereditary right, the will of the people, and the force of arms. Louis–Philippe had not inherited the throne; the people had never been asked to express an opinion about his accession to power; and he was not a military leader or the figurehead of a strong military group. The Orleanist Monarchy was merely a useful compromise that had been clutched at by the desperate owners of property when they feared for their future. Such compromise systems of government depend very much on a leadership that continues to inspire confidence and to convince its supporters that at least it has a moral right to be in power, as the government that is in the best interests of the nation. This was unlikely to go on indefinitely.

Louis–Philippe was unfortunate in that there were ready-made alternative systems of government available. The most widely supported of those was, of course, a republic. It is impossible to estimate with any degree of accuracy how strong the Republicans were in Orleanist France. It seems certain that a large majority of the 'lower orders' were 'natural' Republicans in that they believed a republic would lead to the redress of the ills of poverty and exploitation which afflicted them. These Republicans by sentiment, rather than by membership of a political group, were likely to be active when their material conditions were deteriorating and when they could see no realistic hope of the situation being improved.

There were also a number of Republicans among the 'higher orders' of society. Their number tended to increase with the passing years and with the establishment of a highly romanticized view of the nature of the first French Republic set up as part of the Revolution. This image of the Republic was fostered by sympathetic histories of the period which were published during Louis–Philippe's reign, and by the fact that fewer and fewer people who had experienced the events themselves remained alive. Whereas in 1830 the prospect of a republic had filled the well-to-do with shock and horror, by the mid-1840s there was more of a feeling that perhaps a republic would not be such a bad thing after all.

The other two possible systems of government were supported by only a small minority of French people. Although many of Charles X's supporters had fairly rapidly rallied to Louis–Philippe, a number of them had remained loyal to the legitimist cause. These were joined by some younger men of distinction as the memory of Charles' wrongdoings receded, and as it became increasingly fasionable to adopt a romantic attachment to the idea of the Middle Ages, including the belief that kings were God's representatives on earth. The Legitimists were not notable because of their numbers, but because they were mainly important and able people who could do great damage to the regime by making the most of every hint of scandal and every decision that turned out to be questionable. They helped to create an atmosphere in which it was not socially acceptable to be too obviously in favour of the Orleanist system.

The Bonapartists, on the other hand, seemed in the 1830s to be a spent force, and there seemed no real chance that a new Napoleonic Empire would be established. Napoleon himself had died in exile on St. Helena in 1821, and when his only legitimate son died in 1832 the threat of the Bonaparte family to the established order in France appeared to be at an end. The claimant to the Napoleonic crown was a young man, Louis Napoleon, a nephew of the great Emperor. It was difficult to take his political aspirations seriously, especially after his two attempts at a *coup d'état* in 1836 and 1840 ended in complete failure (see pages 00–00). They seemed to prove that, although the Napoleonic Legend was very much alive in people's minds, it did not stir them to action. Louis-Philippe had good reason to feel that he had nothing to fear from the descendants of his Imperial predecessor. He even attempted to gain reflected glory from the triumphs of the past by sending his son to St. Helena in 1840 to bring back Napoleon's remains for burial. This was clearly the action of a confident man.

Few historical events, however, are inevitable and the fall of Louis–Philippe was not one of them. With historical hindsight it is possible to see that the regime was more likely to fall than to survive, but it was clearly the actions of Louis–Philippe and his ministers, together with an unfortunate combination of developments in 1848, that converted the likelihood into a certainty. Even the King's changing personality and the nature of his private life contributed to a loss of popular support.

* It is said that as you grow older you become more and more like yourself. Louis–Philippe was born in 1773. In 1843 he celebrated his seventieth birthday. He was surprisingly fit and alert for his age but there was no disguising the fact that he had become an old man. The traits which he had exhibited earlier in his life became more and more pronounced in the latter years of his reign. The talkativeness which had been a part of his desire to please became one of the most marked aspects of his personality, but now, instead of flattering those to whom he spoke, his extreme loquacity was an inconvenience to be endured by those who had dealings with him. His rather one-sided conversations were witty and erudite but to younger people, who felt they had little time to waste, they were annoying and frustrating. So was his constant indecision. In the early part of his reign he had taken his time to reach a conclusion; in the 1840s he attempted to avoid making decisions altogether. He pronounced himself satisfied with the way things were and saw no reason why anything should be changed. He had found a chief minister in Guizot who was to his liking and who shared most aspects of his outlook. To Louis-Philippe and Guizot it seemed that the political system was working well and was in need of no reform, that the poor were poor because of factors outside the government's control and that to interfere in matters relating to their conditions would probably make things worse.

As was only to be expected, he became less energetic with advancing years. His public appearances became fewer and were less effective in creating and maintaining the personal loyalties that he had earlier established. After 1840 he ceased reviewing units of the National Guard. Considering the way in which he had used it as the bulwark of his regime this was a significant change and one which considerably weakened his position. He assumed that having once earned their support he would retain it for ever, but he failed to understand that he was leaving a vacuum that might be filled by others when a crisis came. Louis–Philippe was taking too much for granted.

A quiet life with a settled routine appeals to most elderly people but it is not what is generally expected from a leader. It has often been said that Louis–Philippe's life style was such that it left him open to ridicule. He did not play the part of the grand king in the way that was traditional in France. Instead of being waited on hand, foot and finger, he did much for himself. Part of his daily routine was to get up early, shave himself, and make his own fire. Here were three things that people with social pretensions left behind them as soon as possible. They were thought to be hardly the things that a King of France would do. French kings since Louis XIV (who died in 1715) had been remote and inaccessible, to be approached and waited upon only by those of high birth. Louis–Philippe, in contrast, was prepared to receive members of the bourgeoisie as well as aristocrats and to talk to them without great formality. More than this, he was sometimes to be found walking the streets of Paris, unannounced and virtually unattended, in a way that did not conform to normal expectations of regal behaviour.

In the eighteenth and early nineteenth centuries it was the social custom for rulers and members of the ruling class to have a succession of mistresses. The resulting illegitimate children, although barred from succeeding to their father's lands and titles, were normally enobled and well provided for, and were regarded as people of importance. Louis–Philippe had no mistresses. He was a very obviously happily married to a fine women, Marie-Amélie, daughter of the King of Naples, with whom he had had five sons and three daughters, all of whom were a great credit to their parents. Such a harmonious royal family life was almost unparallelled in France or elsewhere before or after the Orleanist Monarchy, with the obvious exception of Queen Victoria. The private lives of the royal family therefore provided little meat for the purveyors of gossip, who, because they needed to attack Louis–Philippe in one way or another, were forced to fall back on the claim that the King was dull and boring. He was ridiculed for being like an ordinary person. His dress was insufficiently distinctive. He lived like a bourgeois merchant or trader with his family clustered around him. He looked undistinguished, being overweight, with sagging jowls that gave rise to the often quoted jibe that his face was shaped like a pear. All in all, it was claimed, he was insufficiently different from the ordinary man in the street to be worth having as a king.

It is difficult to assess how far these personal factors were the causes of the loss of support-suffered by Louis–Philippe in the last years of his reign. Certainly they contributed to the widespread feeling that the July Monarchy had outlived its usefulness and that there would have to be a change of regime if France were to be in a position to continue developing politically. But on their own they would not have caused the collapse of the system. It was only when government policies abroad and at home reinforced the feeling of dull mediocrity without hope of improvement that the situation became desperate for the regime. Many erstwhile supporters became convinced that there was little point in struggling to maintain a system that seemed so negative in its approach. It was not that Louis–Philippe's life style and changing personality turned friends into enemies; rather, they contributed to a slump in morale which left the way open to those who passionately wanted change.

LES POIRES,

Faites à la cour d'assises de Paris par le directeur de la *Caricature*

Vendues pour payer les 6000 fr. d'amende du journal le *Charivari*

Sur la demande d'un grand nombre d'abonnés des départe-
mens, nous donnons aujourd'hui dans le *Charivari* les poires qui
servirent a notre défense, dans l'affaire ou la *Caricature* fût
condamnée à six mois de prison et 2000 fr. d'amende

Si, pour reconnaître le monarque dans une caricature, vous n'attendez pas qu'il soit désigner autrement que par la ressemblance, vous
tomberez dans l'absurde. Voyez ces croquis informes, auxquels j'aurais peut-être dû borner ma défense

Ce croquis ressemble à Louis-Philippe, vous condamnerez donc?

Alors il faudra condamner celui-ci, qui ressemble au premier.

Puis condamner cet autre, qui ressemble au second.

Et enfin, si vous êtes conséquens, vous ne sauriez absoudre cette
poire, qui ressemble aux croquis précédens.

Ainsi, pour une poire, pour une brioche, et pour toutes les têtes grotesques dans lesquelles le hasard ou la malice aura placé cette
triste ressemblance, vous pourrez infliger à l'auteur cinq ans de prison et cinq mille francs d'amende!!
Avouez, Messieurs, que c'est là une singulière liberté de la presse!!

From the Charivari, *1831*

b) Foreign Policy

In foreign affairs, France had been the most powerful nation in Europe for nearly five hundred years. Not all her wars had been successes but it had normally taken a large coalition of other states to bring her to the peace table or to defeat her. French people could hold their heads high in foreign company in the sure knowledge that theirs was a glorious nation with a heroic past. Most recently of all, of course, Napoleon had built up an Empire that at its height had either directly controlled or significantly influenced events throughout most of Europe. This had been achieved by a huge national effort headed by a charismatic leader and a military genius. Fifteen years after the final defeat of Napoleon at the hands of the fourth coalition of European Powers which had been formed against him, Louis–Philippe became King of the French. The people were now ready for France to return to what they regarded as her natural position as the dominant power in Europe.

Louis–Philippe had other ideas. His experiences as a young man seeking refuge abroad, first as revolutionary fervour and then as Napoleonic ambition spilled over into general wars, led him to view an active and independent foreign policy with suspicion. His natural caution and desire for peace were reinforced by the knowledge that the other major European Powers – Austria, Russia, Britain, and to a lesser extent Prussia – were determined not to allow France to endanger the security of other European states again. He strongly suspected that with any provocation the Powers would take the opportunity to impose their will on France as they had in 1815. He was also acutely aware that he was not the legitimate ruler of his country at a time when Austria and Russia especially were playing the part of self-appointed policemen of Europe, ensuring that liberal and revolutionary tendencies were supressed as quickly as possible. It would not have been greatly surprising to Louis–Philippe if the other major European Powers had banded together to force his abdication and the restoration of a legitimate Bourbon King.

Louis–Philippe's firmly held views on foreign policy, therefore, were based on a realistic appraisal of what was possible. It was not what many politicians and most of his people wanted but in the King's mind it was the only option open to him. His overriding aim was to avoid a general European War in which France would be opposed by Austria, Russia, Prussia and Britain. He hoped for friendship with Britain, whose some- what similar form of government made her in many ways a natural ally, because as long as he was working with her the feared combination of Powers against him could not take place. Within this context he was, of course, anxious to gain whatever advantage he could for his country, but not at the risk of failing to achieve his priority aims.

★ Within a month of coming to power his approach to foreign policy was put to the test. The area that is today Belgium had never been an independent country. For centuries it had been a part of one of the great

European Empires – the Spanish, the Austrian and then the French. In the peace treaty of 1815 it was joined to the neighbouring Netherlands to form what it was hoped would be a strong buffer to future French expansion. Unfortunately for the great powers, the Belgians were not happy with the situation, especially disliking the way they were treated as second class citizens by the Dutch. In August 1830 they rebelled and attempted to establish themselves as an independent country. Here was temptation indeed for the French. The boundary between France and the United Netherlands made no sense; it followed no geographical barrier. It divided French speaker from French speaker and it kept France from what she had for a long time regarded as her natural northern frontier, the River Rhine. The fear that France would annex the area was general in Europe. Louis–Philippe refused to do so. Instead he worked as closely as possible with Britain to ensure that Belgium did become independent and that the wish of Austria, Russia and Prussia to see the Netherlands reunited was frustrated. He even refused the throne of the newly independent kingdom for his son despite great pressure in the country to accept. He was in no doubt that a member of the French royal family as King of Belgium would spell the end of the working partnership with Britain and this he was not prepared to sacrifice to dynastic or national ambition.

  * Similar motivation was apparent in his dealings with Spain where rival factions were struggling for power, resulting in a long drawn out but sporadic civil war which provided ample opportunities for outside interference. It might have been reasonable to assume that Spain was clearly in France's sphere of influence. The two countries shared a long common border and no other power had traditionally had great influence there. Yes, because Britain, through Lord Palmerston her Foreign Secretary, was unprepared to see unilateral French action in Spain, Louis–Philippe was careful throughout the 1830s to show that he was not attempting to gain an unfair advantage in the area.

  * Only once was Louis–Philippe forced into a position where a general European War was a strong possibility. The huge Ottoman Empire, covering most of the Balkans, Asia Minor, and the Middle East, had often been unable to maintain its authority to the very limits of its territory. It had regularly fallen back on the expedient of establishing local rulers who were allowed to do much as they liked as long as they respected the general suzerainty of the Sultan in Constantinople. One such local leader was Mehemet Ali in Egypt, who to the displeasure of the Sultan had extended his power and influence in the 1820s until he was almost more powerful than the Sultan himself. This was not to the displeasure of the French who regarded Mehemet Ali as one of their clients, being dependent on French loans, French weapons and French experts in economic and military affairs. The other European Powers were not so happy with the situation. They realized that either an Ottoman Empire shattered by civil war or a revitalized Empire under

Mehemet Ali would upset the balance of power in the Eastern Mediterranean – the gateway to the Black Sea and southern Russia and the pivot
in the route from Britain to her colossal Empire in India. The only
solution to the problem that would satisfy Britain, Russia and, following
them, Austria and Prussia, was for Mehemet Ali to be satisfied with less
territory and less influence over the Ottoman Empire than his force of
arms and his skill as a diplomat and military leader could earn for him.
Mehemet Ali was not prepared to accept this, and nor were the people of
France who saw in the Egyptian leader a man who could at least provide
them with reflected glory.

When the crisis reached a head in 1839–40 Louis–Philippe had been
forced to accept Adolphe Thiers as his leading minister. Thiers was one
of the outstanding politicians of the Orleanist period and had played a
large part in orchestrating the opposition to Charles X in 1830 and in
ensuring that Louis–Philippe was proclaimed king. But the new monarch disliked the way in which Thiers expected him to be a figurehead
rather than a powerful influence in day-to-day politics, and he did his
best to avoid appointing him a minister. This was not always possible,
however, for sometimes other leading politicians were out of favour in
the Assembly leaving only Thiers who could command a majority.
Certainly Thiers was not prepared to allow the King to conduct his own
foreign policy. Instead of ensuring close liaison with Britain, French
policy become obstructionist, attempting to stop the Powers taking any
action so that Mehemet Ali would be free to resolve matters in his own
interests. The policy failed. Palmerston, whose brand of gun boat diplomacy typified the arrogance of much of Britain's nineteenth-century
foreign policy, was determined that Mehemet Ali must be brought into
line and he took a not very secret pleasure in humiliating France in the
process. Britain and Russia co-operated to defeat Mehemet Ali and to
force him to accept terms that were in accordance with their interests.
Thiers had been unwise enough to indicate that this was an issue over
which France would be prepared to go to war, a view shared by the most
vociferous elements in French society. Palmerston called the bluff by
doing just what Thiers has threatened would lead France to declare war
on Mehemet Ali's behalf. Louis–Philippe was therefore left with no
alternative but to replace Thiers and to accept the unavoidable national
humiliation that the aggressive policy had caused because he was not
prepared to fight either Britain or Russia. The public's displeasure was
all heaped on the King as it was clearly seen to be he who had drawn back
from the brink of war when the honourable thing might have been to
stand resolute and accept the consequences. To Louis–Philippe the
unpopularity was a lesser evil than the collapse of the regime which he
felt would be a sure result of any war against other European Powers.

  * In 1841 Palmerston, as a member of the defeated Whig government
lost office in Britain. The new government under Sir Robert Peel was
more keen to work with France than to score points off her. For the next

five years there existed what might be described as an *entente* between Britain and France. The two royal families exchanged successful visits with one another and sound working relationships between the leading politicians in the two countries were established. This partnership bore fruit as Louis–Philippe, secure with Guizot as his chief minister, was able to ensure that a narrow pursuit of French interests was not allowed to cloud the priority need of France not to become isolated once again.

In a spirit of friendliness what could have been an unpleasant confrontation over the control of Tahiti in the South Pacific was avoided in 1844 when the agent who without authority had annexed the island for France was disowned. In a similar way good sense prevailed in the delicate matter of who should marry the young Queen of Spain and her sister, issues which it was thought would vitally affect the two countries' future influence in Spain. While the matter was still unresolved the Peel ministry fell and Palmerston once more became British Foreign Secretary. At once he moved to gain an advantage for Britain. Louis–Philippe, realizing that the alternatives were either being worsted by Britain or gaining an advantage over her, decided to opt for the latter and acted rapidly to secure the marriages that he preferred. The Affair of the Spanish Marriages is normally taken by British historians to show that the French did not value British friendship and were prepared to act treacherously when they thought it was in their interests to do so. Such a judgement not only seems harsh on Louis–Philippe but seems not to accord with the rest of his dealings in foreign affairs.

It is often said that an unsuccessful foreign policy was one of the significant causes of the downfall of the Orleanist Monarchy. It is clear that a glory-hungry nation could not be pleased with what was achieved abroad. The popular wish was for a return to the days when France had been the most powerful and most respected country in Europe, and there was intense frustration generated by the way in which Louis–Philippe seemed to be leading the nation in the opposite direction. To play junior partner to Britain, the traditional enemy, was not thought by most French people to be an honourable role. The fact that this was the best that could be achieved was not widely accepted by a people who yearned for the impossible. Military success in Algeria, which the Orleanist Monarchy achieved at great cost in lives, effort, and money, and which had been possible because it caused conflict with no European Power, was regarded as of little significance. Europe was the area that mattered and here the regime had made no real mark. By 1848 many of those who had supported Louis–Philippe in his early years were thinking that perhaps it was time he gave way to someone else who might do better.

c) Domestic Policy

The domestic policies of Louis–Philippe and his governments were just as disappointing. Once the regime was firmly established and legal ways of dealing with opponents who overstepped the mark, especially in verbal attacks on the government, had been worked out, very little in the way of a positive domestic policy existed. It was the King's view that all that could be done had been done and that there was nothing to gain from tampering with a system that seemed to be working well. Not everybody agreed with him. There was much support for the idea of extending the right to vote for members of the Legislative Assembly. Most Republicans, like the Chartists in Britain, wanted the right to vote to be extended to all men over the age of 21. This was clearly far too extreme to win the support of many in the middle or upper classes who shared with Louis–Philippe the view that the ownership of a significant amount of property was an essential prerequisite for entry to the political process. There were, however, many men who considered themselves to be a part of the social élite who did not have the right to vote. Their active support for the regime might have been won by reforming the system sufficiently to include them within the electorate. Their cause was championed by many in the Legislative Assembly especially Thiers. In the 1840s Guizot had to handle several long and difficult debates on the subject as it became known that neither he nor the King intended to make any changes at all in who had the right to vote. The fact that the Government won the debate shows that the existing electoral system could be well manipulated to give governments comfortable majorities rather than that public opinion was in favour of no change.

d) Short-Term Causes

The period 1830–48 was a period of great reform in Britain. There it was seen that legislation was necessary to take account of some of the huge economic and social changes that were underway in the country. In France there was no such legislative programme. It is true that in France the Industrial Revolution was taking place far more slowly than in either Britain or Belgium, but still there were major changes that seemed to necessitate some government action. Paris, especially, was growing at an enormous rate and this was creating considerable problems of poverty and poor living conditions even when the economy was booming. After 1846, when there was widespread under- and unemployment, the situation was critical. Tens of thousands of poor people were left to exist in misery, depending on charity as and where they could find it. The Government's reaction was to claim that there was nothing they could do about it.

It was not only the poor who were angry at this refusal to accept any responsibility. Ever since 1830 there had been a growing interest among the well-to-do in the 'condition of the people' issue. By the time the economic crisis came in 1846 there was general support for the view that something, however modest, must be done. Louis–Philippe's refusal to change his opinion that there was nothing the Government could do left him increasingly isolated among what should have been the ranks of his natural supporters and completed the disillusionment of many moderate people who in the 1830s had hoped that the July Monarchy would provide a flexible and responsive regime to take France into the second half of the century. Thus, by 1847, Louis–Philippe and his government were so lacking in positive support that they were vulnerable to almost any attack. Unfortunately neither the King nor members of the opposition such as Thiers, who wished to change the ministry not the regime, realized this and so they blundered into a revolution they had not foreseen.

* The short-term causes of the 1848 Revolution in France were not, therefore, nearly as dramatic as the events they precipitated. The political opponents of Guizot within the Assembly had since 1840 tried all sorts of ways to force him out of power and to attain office for themselves. They had no wish to see the King overthrown. In 1847, led by Thiers who was desperately seeking an effective method of agitation as opposition in the Chamber had left the Government unmoved, they held what was to be the first in a series of banquets to champion the cause of electoral reform. The idea was to whip up popular support for their policies by arranging a large number of local meetings at which the strength of their following could be displayed. This idea was borrowed directly from the Anti-Corn Law League in England, where it had been successful in publicizing the widespread support enjoyed by the movement. About seventy banquets were held, but instead of the moderate reformers keeping control of them they were often taken over by extreme Republicans who used them to acquire publicity for their cause and to preach the necessity of overthrowing the regime. All this was taking place against a background of serious economic depression which had reduced the standard of living of the poorer urban classes to near starvation level.

In the circumstances it was not unexpected that the Government took steps to ban the banquets, and the one due to take place in Paris on 22 February 1848 was declared illegal. A march to take its place was organized by the Republicans. When the National Guard, called out to control the crowds, did not seem to be wholeheartedly on the King's side, Louis–Philippe realized that he had misjudged the mood of the country. It was now that his nerve failed him. Instead of standing firm and attempting to weather what was so far only a modest storm, he took fright and dismissed Guizot in an attempt to mollify the opposition. The effect was just the opposite of what he had intended. Instead of weakening the appeal of the agitators the King's action gave increased hope to his enemies who saw that they had forced the regime on to the defensive. It also filled his supporters with dismay because this loss of stubbornness and resoluteness at just the time they were needed most suggested that the end would not be long in coming. Few were prepared to come to the rescue of what already seemed to be a lost cause.

Th decisive event took place the next day when troops fired on what was a fairly good-natured crowd. The eighty dead and wounded were just what the Republican leaders needed to create the anger necessary to mobilize the majority in Paris. The barricades went up and a civil disturbance had become a revolution. Still Louis–Philippe might have saved the day if he had been prepared to use the army, which was still loyal, to put down the rising in Paris, just as he had done in Lyons in 1831 and 1834 when the city had fallen under the control of Republicans following uprisings of discontented workers who were suffering greatly as a result of the economic depression. But the lack of support from the National Guard, which he had regarded as the bulwark of his regime, seems to have destroyed his will to continue. The army was not ordered to move, and on 24 February 1848 Louis-Philippe abdicated and began his flight, in disguise, to England and exile once again.

The events of 22–24 February were not such that they should have toppled the regime, even allowing for the fact that widespread unemployment and extreme poverty had created in Paris a situation that was almost certain to erupt in violence. A well-supported and resolute government would have imposed its will on the capital. As was said at the time, 'The Government was not overthrown, it was allowed to fall'. It was not just in Louis–Philippe that people had lost faith. If it had been, his attempt to abdicate in favour of his grandson, the nine-year-old comte de Paris, would have been successful. The feeling was widely held that here was a regime that was based on nothing but greed and self-interest. It could not claim to be based on tradition nor on the will of the people, and its supporters became increasingly uncomfortable under the endless gibes of its opponents. Confidence was destroyed, and without that the July Monarchy of Louis–Philippe was vulnerable to almost any attack. The experiment in constitutional monarchy had failed.

e) Conclusion

Most historians would agree that the factors described above are the important causes of the 1848 Revolution in France. They would, however, be less prepared to accept any one judgment about the relative significance of the factors. Marxist historians, who accept Karl Marx's general interpretation of history as essentially comprising a series of 'class struggles', argue that the revolution took place because the proletariat (the urban working class) felt ready to seize the political control of society from the bourgeoisie (the propertied middle classes). They therefore stress the particular importance of economic and social factors and argue that the actions of individuals, such as Louis–Philippe and Guizot, were largely incidental, merely supplying the occasion for what was inevitably to take place.

Another general interpretation is supplied by historians steeped in the traditions of French political activity since 1789 who view the events of

1848 as part of a single long-term revolution starting in the late
eighteenth century and continuing well into the twentieth century. The
theme of their revolution is seen as being the destruction of privilege and
the growth of liberty. Thus 1848 is interpreted as being an attempt to
continue the unfinished work of 1789, caused by 'general political forces'
rather than by the actions of named individuals.

The tendency is for historical interpretations relying on general theories to be produced more frequently in continental Europe than in
Britain, where most historians are used to explaining causation in terms
of particular events and situations rather than in terms of general trends
and movements. This is partly because highly educated people in
Britain, among whom historians must be numbered, are traditionally
suspicious of explanations that claim to provide simple answers to
complicated and wide-ranging questions. So the 'orthodox' view in
Britain about the February Revolution is that it was caused by the
complex interaction of a large number of factors, which are described
earlier in the chapter, and that we have insufficient evidence to claim that
any one factor was significantly more important than the others. Such a
standpoint can be seen as either an overcautious refusal to come off the
fence, or a responsible reluctance to stretch the evidence further than one
ought.

It was the standpoint adopted by Alexis de Tocqueville when he
attempted to explain what had happened in his *Recollections,* written only
two years after the event. Tocqueville had been at the centre of French
political life for many years and had experienced the Revolution at first
hand. In trying to make sense of what had happened he wrote:

1 The Revolution of February, in common with all other great events
of this class, sprang from general causes, impregnated, if I am
permitted the expression, by accidents; and it would be as superfi-
cial a judgment to ascribe it necessarily to the former or exclusively
5 to the latter.

The industrial revolution which, during the past thirty years,
had turned Paris into the principal manufacturing city of France
and attracted within its walls an entire new population of workmen
tended more and more to inflame this multitude. Add to this the
10 democratic disease of envy, which was silently permeating it; the
economical and political theories which were beginning to make
their way and which strove to prove that human misery was the
work of laws and not of Providence, and that poverty could be
suppressed by changing the conditions of society; the contempt
15 into which the governing class, and espevially the men who led it,
had fallen, a contempt so general and so profound that it paralyzed
the resistance even of those who were most interested in maintaining the power that was being overthrown; the centralization which
the overmastering of Paris and the seizing of the machinery of

20 government; and lastly, the mobility of all this, institutions, ideas,
men and customs, in a fluctuating state of society which had, in less
than sixty years, undergone the shock of seven great revolutions,
without numbering a multitude of smaller, secondary upheavals.
These were the general causes without which the Revolution of
25 February would have been impossible. The principal accidents
which led to it were the passions of the dynastic Opposition, which
brought about a riot in proposing a reform; the suppression of this
riot, first over-violent and then abandoned; the sudden dis-
appearance of the old Ministry, unexpectedly snapping the threads
30 of power, which the new ministers, in their confusion, were unable
either to seize upon or to reunite; the mistakes and disorder of mind
of these ministers, so powerless to re-establish that which they had
been strong enough to overthrow; the vacillation of the generals;
the absence of the only princes who possessed either
35 personal energy or popularity; and above all, the senile imbecility
of King Louis–Philippe, his weakness, which no one could have
foreseen, and which still remains almost incredible, after the event
has proved it.

Making notes on 'Louis–Philippe, 1830–48'

Your notes on the period 1830–48 should help you to understand the
nature of the changes that took place in 1830, and the reasons why
Louis–Philippe became king and was able to consolidate his position.
They should also give you a framework for discussing the reasons for
Louis–Philippe's fall in 1848.

The following headings and sub-headings should assist you:

1.   The regime established
1.1.   Why did Louis–Philippe become king?
1.2.   Louis–Philippe, the man
1.3.   Changes in the political system
2.   The regime consolidated
3.   The fall of the regime
3.1.   Long-term causes
3.1.1. Basic weaknesses of regime
3.1.2. Attitudes and actions of Louis–Philippe
3.1.3. Foreign policy
3.1.4. Domestic policy
3.2.   Short-term causes
3.3.   Conclusion

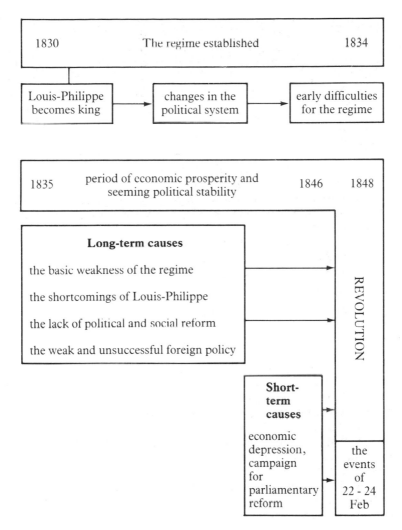

Summary – Louis–Philippe, 1830–48

Answering essay questions on 'Louis–Philippe, 1830–48'

You will at some stage be expected to use evidence from this chapter in helping to answer general questions on the period 1814–70. A discussion of these questions is given on pages 130–131.

Essay questions which are limited to the period 1830–48 tend to concentrate on one issue: The causes of the 1848 Revolution. Typical questions are:

'How far do economic factors explain the collapse of the July Monarchy in France?' (AEB, 1982)

'To what extent was the overthrow of Louis–Philippe in 1848 the result of defects in his own character and outlook?' (SUJB, 1979)

' "Domestic, not Foreign, issues were the causes of the down fall of the Orleanist monarchy in 1848." Do you accept this view?' (Cambridge, 1981)

Make a list of the factors you think were important in causing the 1848 Revolution in France. Organize your list into groups. You might arrange according to a chronological framework, with groups of *long-term, short-term* and *immediate causes*. You might prefer to use groupings by topic, such as *economic, social* and *political*. You might even be able to combine both approaches and produce a quite sophisticated table of causes.

Any essay on the causes of the 1848 Revolution in France should contain reference to all the factors you have listed. But the order and method of presentation of the factors will depend entirely on the wording of the question asked.

Notice that all three questions above require you to comment on the *relative* importance of the causes. So it is vital that you have clear opinions on which factors were of greater significance than others. On the list or table you have drawn up, indicate the importance of the factors by numbering them, 1, 2, 3 etc. Try not to end up with more than two factors being of equal importance.

You are now in a good position to answer any of the three questions. After a brief introduction, it is usually best to start with the factor or factors mentioned in the question. Describe and assess the importance of the factor(s), taking special care to make links with the detailed wording of the question. Then deal with the other factors in what seems the most appropriate order. You can decide this by working from either the least to the most important factor, or vice versa.

Using this approach, make an essay plan for each of the three questions. For one of the plans, add after each paragraph heading the evidence that you would include to support your argument.

Source-based questions on 'Louis–Philippe, 1830–48'

1 The character of Louis–Philippe

Read carefully the report on Louis–Philippe given on page 39, the pen-portrait given on page 40, and look carefully at the cartoon reproduced on page 49. Answer the following questions:
a) What is the main general criticism that the author of the pen-portrait has to make of Louis–Philippe?
b) The two pieces of written evidence give contradictory general impressions of Louis–Philippe. Give several reasons that might explain why this is so.
c) What were likely to have been the motives of the artist who drew the cartoon? Use evidence from the cartoon to justify your answer.
d) What facets of Louis–Philippe's character and personality do all three sources substantiate directly or indirectly?

2 The placard of 1830

Read carefully the wording of the placard given on pages 40–41. Answer the following questions:
a) What evidence is there that the men who designed the placard held moderate political views?
b) Why does the placard refer to events that took place more than thirty years previously?
c) What are the implications of the last line of the placard?

3 The causes of the 1848 Revolution

Read carefully the extract from Alexis de Tocqueville's *Recollections* given on pages 57–58, and answer the following questions:
a) Explain the meaning and significance of i) 'democratic disease of envy' (line 10); and ii) 'centralisation' (line 17).
b) What does Tocqueville consider to have been the effect of the dismissal of Guizot's ministry?
c) What evidence is there that Tocqueville's view of Louis–Philippe is unbalanced?
d) What significant causes of the Revolution does Tocqueville *not* mention?

CHAPTER 4

The Second Republic, 1848–52

1 The Establishment of the Republic

The abdication of Louis–Philippe left a vacuum of power and authority. The Legislative Assembly, which was in session at the time, would willingly have declared a regency for the ex-King's grandson had not the Republicans inside and outside the Assembly acted speedily. A part of the armed mob which had caused the abdication was organized to burst into the Chamber of Deputies as the arrangements for the succession were being discussed and to prevent anything being done. The mob was successful. Most of the Deputies fled, and to those who remained it was clear that only the declaration of a republic would calm things down.

The leading Republican in the Assembly was Lamartine whose reputation was based on his popular poetry and on his considerable gifts of oratory. Together with a handful of other Deputies with Republican sympathies, Lamartine decided to declare a republic and to form a provisional government. Others had the same idea: at exactly the same time the journalists of the major Republican newspapers, who were also about to declare a provisional government of the republic, were deciding on whom to invite to form the new government. Both sets of people were romantics and idealists who believed that with the revolution that was taking place the age of human happiness based on liberty, equality and fraternity was about to dawn. There was therefore, surprisingly little animosity between the various groups of Republicans.

Lamartine and his fellow Deputies hurried to the *hôtel de ville* where the first French Republic had been declared, and where the journalists were preparing to respond to the crowd which was demanding a republic. Agreement was speedily reached and Lamartine and the Deputies joined with the journalists and their associates to form one provisional government to head the new republic which Lamartine was chosen to declare in traditional form from the balcony of the *hôtel de ville*. The crowd was delighted and noisily showed their acceptance of the names of each of the people put forward to be members of the provisional government. Although the following days were filled with widespread rumours of attacks on the rich and their property, there was much less violence than might have been expected. The poor were suffering greatly and the forces of law and order were ill-equipped to resist them. But no general uprising of the 'lower orders' took place. There was a feeling evident in Paris that victory had been won and all would now be well.

* It is usually a fact that the forces which combine to overthrow a regime are united by their opposition to what exists rather than by any detailed agreement about the policies to be pursued in the future. This was the case in France in 1848. Strongly represented among the organizers of revolutionary activity in Paris were those who came to be

called the Red Republicans. Their leading spokesman was Ledru-Rollin, one of the Deputies who had become a member of the Provisional Government. The Red Republicans wanted social change as well as political change. They felt strongly about the conditions in which the poor in the large towns and cities had to exist. Housing was poor, even by mid-nineteenth century standards; public utilities, such as sanitation and the supply of water, were rudimentary if they existed at all. Even those with paid employment had hardly enough money to pay the rent on their room or rooms and to buy sufficient food to prevent a slow starvation from overcoming them. The many thousands of unemployed and their families barely existed by begging and borrowing for there was no system of providing financial assistance to those who had no work.

The main solution advocated by the Red Republicans was to ensure 'le droit au travail', the right to work, for everybody, so that the extremes of poverty would be avoided. Jobs were to be created by an ambitious programme of public works which, in part, would be aimed at improving environmental conditions in the towns and cities. Such public works, of course, would have to be paid for by increased taxation which would overwhelmingly fall on the property-owning classes in society such as the peasant landowners, the middle classes and the aristocracy.

The most influential supporters of the new Republic were members of the middle and upper classes, a large majority of whom feared the aspirations of the Red Republicans. What nowadays would seem a modest degree of social reform was viewed in 1848 as an unwarranted attack on the rights of property, for more well-to-do Republicans wished for no extension of state intervention in the lives of individuals, believing that the owners of property should be free to use it as they wished. They were alarmed at the prospect of any increase in taxation and they had little general sympathy for the poor whom they regarded as being mainly feckless, irresponsible, and immoral, and as such largely the cause of their own misfortunes. The middle-class fear of the urban rabble was clearly evident in the months after the February Revolution, and it was the major factor in dividing and weakening the potential support for the new regime.

* Yet most Republicans were united in support of one element of political reform. Universal manhood suffrage – the right of every man over the age of 21 to vote in elections – was a traditional objective for Republicans. It was Louis–Philippe's refusal to agree to an extension of the franchise which had lost him so much support in the last years of his reign, and once a republic had been declared it was certain that the desire to return to a system of 'one man, one vote' would be gratified. A declaration of universal manhood suffrage was in fact the first act of the Provisonal Government. The second action was to declare 'le droit au travail' and this was followed by a decision to raise a supplementary tax, mainly falling on the landowning classes, to pay for it.

Just as the move to universal manhood suffrage was almost a certainty, so it was inconceivable that in the Paris of February 1848 *'le droit au travail'* would be refused. With widespread starvation imminent and social unrest so apparent, the first priority of the property-owning classes was to buy off those whose discontent could so easily have boiled over into general, destructive civil commotion. To give way over the right to work had the added advantage to those who wanted as few changes as possible that it diverted the Red Republicans' attention from other schemes that were potentially more harmful to the men of property. Once the right to work had been conceded an immense amount of time and energy was given to trying to convert theory into practice, for there was little work immediately available for the tens of thousands of the unemployed in Paris.

The Red Republican members of the Provisional Government spent weeks trying to organize National Workshops in which the unemployed would serve. But without practical experience of organizing on such a scale, and without a large body of administrators to back them up, it is not surprising that only a few ventures actually commenced. Most of those whose names were on the lists of the unemployed were merely given a small weekly payment, for there was no work for them to do. Even the most radical members of the Provisional Government recognized that there was not an endless supply of money to hand out to the poor, and it was decided that once the lists were full no futher names would be added. Thus 120 000 were in receipt of the 'dole', with an unknown number – perhaps 50 000 – left unprovided for.

a) The Constituent Assembly, 1848–9

While the National Workshops were being organized the Provisional Government got on with the task it had set itself of organizing the election of a Constituent Assembly whose duty it would be to draw up a constitution for the new republic. There was in France a long tradition of placing official pressure on the electorate in order to secure the return of candidates who would support the government. But the situation under universal manhood suffrage was much more difficult to manage for instead of 200 000 electors there were now over eight million. Although the Provisional Government attempted to influence events by appointing known supporters as Prefects and Sub-Prefects, the local government officials through whom the pressure was applied, the task of 'educating' the mass of peasant farmers who made up the large majority of the voting population could not be undertaken effectively in this way. To make matters worse for those who hoped to see Deputies elected who would favour a radical republic, it was decided to hold the elections on Easter Sunday. In retrospect this seems a strange decision, for in many villages the priest, having preached against the evils of Red Republicanism, led his faithful flock to vote. But even without this error of judgement the Provisional Government would have been faced by a conservative

Assembly because it was well known that the great fear of the peasant farmers was that a radical government would attempt to weaken their hold on the ownership of the land. Tocqueville found this when he returned home to present himself as a candidate in the election:

1 As every one knows, the Department of La Manche is peopled almost exclusively by farmers. It contains few large towns, few manufacturers, and, with the exception of Cherbourg, no places in which workmen are gathered in large numbers. At first, the Revo-
5 lution was hardly noticed there. The upper classes immediately bent beneath the blow, and the lower classes scarcely felt it. Generally speaking, agricultural populations are slower than others in perceiving, and more stubborn in retaining, political impressions; they are the last to rise and the last to settle down again. The
10 steward of my estate, himself half a peasant, describing what was taking place in the country immediately after the 24th February, wrote:
    "People here say that if Louis–Philippe has been sent away, it is a good thing, and that he deserved it. . . ."
15   This was to them the whole moral of the play. But when they heard tell of the disorder reigning in Paris, of the new taxes to be imposed, and of the general state of war that was to be feared; when they saw commerce cease and money seem to sink down into the ground, and when, in particular, they learnt that the principle
20 of property was being attacked, they did not fail to perceive that there was something more than Louis–Philippe in question.
    Fear, which had first displayed itself in the upper circles of society, then descended into the depths of the people, and universal terror took possession of the whole country. This was the
25 condition in which I found it when I arrived about the middle of March. I was at once struck by a spectacle that both astonished and charmed me. A certain demagogic agitation reigned, it is true, among the workmen in the towns; but in the country all the landed proprietors, whatever their origin, antecedents, education or
30 means, had come together, and seemed to form but one class: all former political hatred and rivalry of caste or fortune had disappeared from view. There was no more jealousy or pride displayed between the peasant and the squire, the nobleman and the commoner; instead, I found mutual confidence, reciprocal
35 friendliness, and regard. Property had become, with all those who owned it, a sort of bond of fraternity. The wealthy were the elder, the less endowed the younger brothers; but all considered themselves members of one family, having the same interest in defending the common inheritance.

In the event over half the Deputies elected were Monarchists rather than Republicans, and only a small minority were Red Republicans and supporters of Ledru-Rollin's. So the work of drawing up a constitution was entrusted to men who were largely not in favour of the system of government they were creating. That a Republican constitution emerged was, of course, the result of the hopeless split between those Monarchists who wanted a restoration of a Bourbon King (the Legitimists), and those who championed the grandson of Louis–Philippe (the Orleanists).

b) The June Days

Emboldened by the settled state of Paris brought about by the payment of the 'dole' by the National Workshops, and by the conservative nature of the Constituent Assembly, the moderate Republicans in the Provisional Government decided that the time was right to assert the dominance of the men of property and to put the masses back in their 'proper' place. It was decided to end the system of National Workshops which was costing so much money and which was having the effect of attracting large numbers of the poorest classes of society from all over the country to Paris in the hope of receiving a hand-out from the Government. However, the unemployed were not to be left unprovided for. The unmarried men among them were to be drafted into the army and the married men and their families were to go into the provincies where, it was promised by the Government, work would be found for them. The motives of the moderate Republicans in the Government are easy to understand. They felt threatened by the presence of so large a number of able-bodied, and potentially revolutionary, poor in Paris and were determined to disperse them in one way or another. The army was known to be loyal to the Government and it was planned that if the poor resisted the new regulations they would be forced into compliance.

There was a widespread reaction from the Paris poor to the Government's instructions. There was no need for agitators to stir up trouble; the traditional barricades were erected in all the poorer quarters of Paris, and a large number of rioters, mostly armed, took to the streets. This was a more determined resistance, – known as the June Days, – than had caused the downfall of Louis–Philippe five months previously. But the situation was now very different. The Government had engineered the situation and was quite prepared to use whatever force was necessary to impose its will. With calculated and cold-hearted efficiency General Cavaignac, who had been given the duty of restoring law and order in the capital, brought up his troops and their field guns and once he had assembled overwhelming forces began the task of sweeping away the barricades street by street. As is to be expected in this form of fighting, those behind the barricades suffered fewer casualties than those attacking them (perhaps 500 insurgents killed compared with 1000 troops), but in the mopping up operation that followed the balance was

more than redressed. Troops roamed the quarters in which the barricades had been and killed anybody whom they thought had been
involved in the fighting against them. It was this bloody aftermath, in
which several thousand civilian deaths occurred, which made the June
Days of 1848 a landmark in what the Marxists have seen as the struggle
between the proletariat and the capitalist classes. Thousands more were
imprisoned or deported to penal settlements abroad as the Government
tried to ensure that no potential leaders of the Paris poor would remain to
stir up trouble in the future. Tocqueville was in no doubt about the
long-term significance of the uprising:

1 What distinguished it also, among all the events of this kind which
   have succeeded one another in France for sixty years, is that it did
   not aim at changing the form of government, but at altering the
   order of society. It was not, strictly speaking, a political stuggle, in
5 the sense which until then we had given to the word, but a struggle
   of class against class, a sort of Servile War. It represented the facts
   of the Revolution of February in the same manner as the theories of
   Socialism represented its ideas; or rather it issued naturally from
   these ideas, as a son does from his mother. We behold in it nothing
10 more than a blind and rude, but powerful, effort on the part of the
   workmen to escape from the necessities of their condition, which
   had been depicted to them as one of unlawful oppression, and to
   open up by main force a road towards that imaginary comfort with
   which they had been deluded. It was this mixture of greed and false
15 theory which first gave birth to the insurrection and then made it so
   formidable. These poor people had been told that the wealth of the
   rich was in some way the produce of a theft practised upon themselves. They had been assured that the inequality of fortunes was as
   opposed to morality and the welfare of society as it was to nature.
20 Prompted by their needs and their passions, many had believed
   this obscure and erroneous notion of right, which, mingled with
   brute force, imparted to the latter an energy, a tenacity and a power
   which it would never have possessed unaided.
     It must also be observed that this formidable insurrection was
25 not the enterprise of a certain number of conspirators, but the
   revolt of one whole section of the population against another.

The June Days were also a landmark in the short-term, for after the
four days of terrible violence the nature of the Republic was clear for all
to see. Over were the days when Republicans of all shades of opinion
worked together to bring about the age of enlightenment that was
believed to be about to dawn. Harsh reality had re-asserted itself as the
self-confidence of the propertied classes had returned, and the 'haves' in
society had made it clear that they were not prepared to share with the
'have nots'. The Republic was now the tool by which those who felt they

had a material stake in the country were going to ensure that their assets were well defended.

Had General Cavaignac wished to become a dictator in France he could have done so in June 1848. The army was obedient to his commands and the infant Republic had few active supporters. Yet the regime lived on, for Cavaignac was one of the relatively small group of men who still had faith in Republican forms of government based on the will of the people, as exercised in elections held under universal manhood suffrage. He ensured that law and order were maintained while the Constituent Assembly carried on with its work of drawing up the Constitution.

c) The Constitution

On 4 November 1848 the new Constitution was agreed by the Assembly. Its twin pillars were 'one man, one vote' and a desire to ensure that no one person or institution would become too powerful. Given the élitist attitudes of many of the Deputies it is somewhat surprising that universal manhood suffrage was not hedged about with restrictions that would limit the vote in practice. This might have been because the innate conservatism of the rural masses was recognized, or because it was seen that the urban poor to whom the Red Republicans were likely to appeal were a tiny minority of the total population. But it suggests that some of the ideals that impelled France towards a Republican form of government were still widely held. The significance of the decision should not be underestimated. Since Napoleon had been finally defeated in 1815 no European country had encouraged the ordinary people to play a part in the political process. Even in Britain, which was considered to have a very liberal constitution, the vote was restricted to those who had sufficient wealth to be thought to have shares in the country. For France to opt for universal manhood suffrage in 1848 was to risk being 'sent to Coventry' by the powers of Europe in much the same way as was the Communist Government of Russia after 1917.

The desire to prevent any one person or institution dominating the country was both a reflection of the wish to avoid the emergence of a dictator such as Napoleon which had happened with the First Republic, and a sign that current political ideas, such as those about a division of power, were very influential. The arrangements that were made were as theoretically ideal as could have been devized at the time. Power was divided between a single-chamber Legislative Assembly which would make the laws, and a President who would carry them out. The regulation that no one could serve more than one four-year term as President was intended to ensure that no leader would develop long-term ambitions. As with the size of the electorate, these provisions were very radical for their time.

The absence of a second chamber of the Legislative Assembly, such as a House of Lords or a Chamber of Notables, meant that no special place was reserved for those who were socially, economically, or intellectually pre eminent in the country. The system of electing a President directly by popular vote also reduced the influence of the propertied classes, which might have been protected by arranging, for instance, for the President to be chosen by the Deputies in the Legislative Assembly. Instead of protecting their own narrow interests, the Deputies in the Constituent Assembly attempted to bring into being a political system that truly reflected the aspirations of liberty, equality, and fraternity that had motivated the first French Republicans, as the wording of the Preamble of the Constitution shows:

1 In the presence of God and in the name of the French people, the National Assembly proclaims:

I. France has become a Republic. The aim of adopting this form of government in perpetuity is to move more freely along the road
5 of progress and civilisation, to bring about an increasingly equitable division of society's burdens and benefits, to increase the prosperity of all by the gradual reduction of public expenditure and taxes, and bring all citizens, without further upheavals, . . . to an ever higher state of morality, enlightenment and well-being.
10 II. The French Republic is democratic, one and indivisible.

III. It recognizes rights and duties older and higher than written laws.

IV. Its principles are Liberty, Equality and Fraternity. It is based on the family, work, property and public order.
15 V. It respects other nations, as it expects to be respected by them, does not undertake wars of conquest, and never uses force against the liberty of another people.

VI. Reciprocal duties oblige all citizens to support the Republic, and the Republic to support all citizens.
20 VII. All citizens must love their country, serve the Republic, defend it at the cost of their lives, share in the expenses of government in proportion to their wealth; they must provide for their present needs by working, and for the future by foresight; they must strive for communal well-being by helping one another,
25 and for public order by observing the moral and written laws which govern society, the family, and the individual.

VIII. The Republic must protect the citizen's person, family, religion, property and work, and provide all with the opportunity to receive that education which is necessary for all men; it must . . .
30 look after the needy either by finding them work within the limits of its resources, or by providing, if the family can not, help to those who are unable to work.

In the Constitution were sown the seeds of the Republic's destruction, for the delicate balance which was envisaged could only be maintained if all involved wished to make it work. As soon as anybody put personal power or influence above the good of the system, difficulties were likely to emerge that would throw the continued existence of the Republic into doubt.

2 The Emergence of Louis Napoleon

The Constituent Assembly decreed that the first elections for President would take place in December 1848. In the days before radio, television, and national newspapers, when there were few railways and horse-power provided the main means of transport, when the postal system was in the early stages of development, and the majority of the population was essentially illiterate, it was an impossible task for the candidates in the Presidental election to make effective contact with more than a tiny minority of the vast electorate. Such a situation was tailor-made for anybody whose name was well known and whose image was right, because there were no large scale political parties with an organization in the localities that could harness votes in favour of a chosen candidate. None of the leading candidates was in a position to fight what today would be thought of as a well-organized campaign. Only one tried – Louis Napoleon Bonaparte – who spent a large part of his personal fortune in paying for what must have been one of the earliest attempts at image building on a national scale. Local newspapers were prevailed upon to print articles which reflected well on him, a large-scale poster campaign was launched, and badges, pictures, and Napoleonic momentos were widely distributed. In no part of France should anybody have been ignorant of the fact that Louis Napoleon was the nephew of the great Napoleon and had come to claim what he regarded as his birth right.

The results of the election were decisive. Lamartine who had expected to do quite well, secured less than 19 000 votes in the whole of France. It is true that his reputation had suffered by his association with the actions of the Provisional Government which had managed to give deep offence to both the 'haves' and the 'have nots', but the main explanation for his poor showing must lie in the change of mood that had taken place during 1848. The dreamy, romantic idealism that Lamartine represented was no longer so attractive now that it was apparent that the departure of Louis–Philippe had done nothing to alter the harsh practical realities of life in France. It was generally agreed that what was now needed was a man of action. Ledru-Rollin could claim to be such a man, but he was fatally linked in the minds of the people with the Red Republicans, and although he received much support in the large towns and cities he had hardly a friend in the rural areas, where most of the French population lived. He received only a little over a third of a million votes.

When the coming election for President was announced, and when it was known that General Cavaignac would be a candidate, many assumed that the result was a foregone conclusion. After the June Days the name of Cavaignac was known nationwide. To the conservative-minded rural population here was a man of very definite action who had already shown that he was not prepared to see the rights of property trampled on. By his actions, both in dealing with the Paris mob and in refusing to take personal advantage of the military power that had been placed in his hands, he had won the respect and admiration of many of the property-owners, large and small, who saw in him a man who would maintain law and order while safeguarding political liberty. But his candidature was bitterly resented in some quarters, especially by the millions of people who regarded themselves as being economically exploited by someone else and who therefore tended to identify with the insurgents of the June Days rather than with the forces of law and order that had so brutally crushed them. If there had not been another strong candidate who appealed to those who feared social strife and social disorder, Cavaignac would probably have received a majority of the votes cast despite his obvious drawbacks. In the event nearly one and a half million people voted for him. The triumph, though, was Louis Napoleon's. He received nearly five and a half million votes, more than three times the number of his nearest rival, and well over the 50 per cent of total votes cast needed to secure his election. The reasons for his success are readily explicable, but the victory was still a little breathtaking given Louis Napoleon's previous attempts to gain power and the speed with which he had emerged as a serious contender for the Presidency.

* Charles Louis Napoleon Bonaparte, popularly known as Prince Louis Napoleon, was born in 1808. He was the son of Louis Bonaparte who had been created King of Holland in 1808 by his brother Napoleon, Emperor of France. Hence he was the nephew of the most powerful man in Europe.But the fortunes of the Bonaparte family seemed to be ruined when Napoleon was finally defeated at Waterloo in 1815. Yet, although Napoleon himself was kept in captivity on the island of St Helena until his death in 1821, the remaider of the large Bonaparte family was allowed to live in comfort in Europe outside France and to retain a large amount of the wealth they had acquired during the period of the family's dominance. Louis Napoleon lived with his mother in South Germany and Switzerland, while his father and elder brother lived in Italy. During the formative years of his childhood and adolescence he developed a deep sense of destiny, coming to believe fervently that it was he who would restore the family's fortunes and re-establish them in their rightful place as leaders of France. This was somewhat surprising as Louis Napoleon was in no sense the heir apparent to his uncle. The son of Napoleon I and his own elder brother, both had a prior claim to be the heir to the Bonapartist cause until their deaths in 1832 and 1831. The continued existence of some of Napoleon's brothers, including his own father,

Louis, was of less importance to Louis Napoleon for they had clearly given up all pretensions to reviving the family's fortunes.

The trials and tribulations that beset the Prince as he tried to lay claim to his inheritance would have discouraged anybody who did not possess the blind faith of a fanatic. Not only were the aristocratic circles of Europe in which he moved unsympathetic, and often hostile, to his cause, but the people of France seemed unprepared to take action to restore their country to its former glory. Yet Louis Napoleon's belief in his own destiny remained unshaken despite his setbacks. Most historians have poured scorn on his näive attempts to seize power in France by starting uprisings at Strasbourg in 1836 and Boulogne in 1840, but it must be remembered that the first Napoleon had regained power on returning from exile on Elba in 1815 in almost exactly the same way. What Louis Napoleon had failed to realize was that others' valuation of him was not nearly as high as the regard he had for himself. After the Strasbourg attempt, when efforts to bribe the garrison of this fortress town to mutiny in favour of the Bonapartist cause almost completely failed, the authorities did no more than send the young conspirator back to his footloose exile. When he seemed to misjudge Louis–Philippe's leniency as weakness and attempted a second uprising at Boulogne, the reaction was different. A sentence of imprisonment for life in the fortress of Ham, near the Belgian border, was meted out.

For nearly six years Louis Napoleon lived the life of a prisoner, and although he was treated as a person of importance, being allowed books, writing materials, and equipment with which to carry out scientific experiments, as well as regular visits from a servant girl who bore him two sons, his confinement was closely surpervised and his quarters were cold and damp. When he gained his freedom in 1846 by disguising himself as a workman and walking out of the fortress with a plank over his shoulder in an escape that was as carefully planned as most of those from prisoner of war camps between 1940 and 1945, his health had been permanently damaged, and those who knew him well felt that he had aged by ten years or more. He was, however, fit enough to make quite a name for himself in London high society once he managed to escape across the Channel to England.

* Yet his years in prison had not been wasted. Louis Napoleon's belief in his own destiny was not a simple matter of believing that he should rule France because of who he was. To become ruler of France was a means to an end, not an end in itself. Louis Napoleon wished to carry on the work of his uncle which war and final defeat had prevented being completed. While in exile on St Helena, Napoleon I had talked and written much about what he would have done as leader of France had the allied Powers not imposed a state of almost continual war on the country. It was around those plans, which many impartial commentators have accused Napoleon of dreaming up in retrospect, as much as around memories of glorious military successes, that the Napoleonic Legend had grown up in

France. Napoleon I claimed that his intention had been to liberalize his regime so that the people would have a much greater say in decisions, and that the re-arrangement of society would have continued so as to give further protection to the ordinary people as opposed to people of wealth, rank, and ability. It was on the twin pillars of 'the will of the people' and 'the condition of the people question' that Louis Napoleon built his ideas of the type of France he would like to bring about. His views on 'the will of the people' were very much reinforced by what he saw happening under Louis–Philippe. He saw France as being weak and without a sense of direction, a situation brought about by the political system which encouraged wrangles between parties and factions rather than stressing the issues upon which most French people agreed and acting decisively over them. He felt that what was needed was strong leadership. This should be above party or faction, and should appeal to the mass of ordinary people.

Louis Napoleon's political views were explained fully in his book *Des Idées Napoléoniennes* published in 1839. In it he wrote:

1 Under the empire (of Napoleon I) all the best brains and the talents of France worked to one end, the prosperity of the country. Since then the most intelligent have been busy fighting amongst themselves, arguing about the way to go rather than moving on.
5 Political discipline has been broken so that, instead of marching ahead in a straight line everybody sets up his own line of march and has fallen away from the main body.

The message was clear and has been echoed many times since in countries where attempts at parliamentary democracy have resulted in weak governments and the subsequent emergence of a strong leader stressing discipline and obedience.

While he was a prisoner in the Ham fortress, Louis Napoleon studied and wrote extensively. He became particularly interested in the current concern to find a strategy for doing away with poverty, and his thoughts were published as a book under the somewhat idealistic title of *L'Extinction du Paupérisme*. This, in common with his other writings, was sold in huge numbers throughout France, thanks to carefully planned marketing techniques such as selling at an artificially low subsidized price.

* By February 1848 when Louis–Philippe was overthrown, a large amount of propaganda had been circulated and relatively large sums of money had been spent on promoting the name and claims of Louis Napoleon. But it had been successful in doing little more than creating an awareness of who he was and what he stood for. He did have small numbers of fervent supporters in many localities, but they were not linked together into any national organization. There was no Bonapartist party. It therefore required little courage on the part of the new

Provisional Government to ask Louis Napoleon to leave France after he had made a hurried return from England on hearing of the Revolution. It was not that the new Government saw him as a great threat; merely that he was an annoying complication at a time when they had more than enough to be thinking about. Louis Napoleon withdrew, having the good sense to see that his position was weak and that he would damage his future prospects if he attempted to force the issue. He had clearly learnt something from Strasbourg in 1836 and Boulogne in 1840. He even declined to take his place in the Constituent Assembly, to which he had been elected, when it was made clear to him that his presence in Paris would still not be welcomed by the leaders of the Republic.

Thus Louis Napoleon played no part directly or indirectly in the infamous June Days. This was a huge bonus to a man who aspired to be all things to all people and who would have found himself wishing to support both sides in the struggle to gain control of the Republic. General Cavaignac had gained fame but had made many enemies; Ledru-Rollin had lost all hope of gaining significant support outside the large cities and industrial areas; Louis Napoleon's reputation, such as it was, remained untarnished. The atmosphere within the Republic was sufficiently changed for Louis Napoleon to be able to take his place in the Constituent Assembly when he was successful in the fresh elections that were held in September 1848.

In the Assembly Louis Napoleon made a poor impression. He was a very poor public speaker, having had almost no experience of it; he spoke French with a German accent which added credibility to the charge that he was in essence a foreigner; and he cut a somewhat comic figure with the size of his head accentuated by ferocious looking moustaches, a body of normal proportions, and legs that seemed to be at least one size too short. As well as this, he seemed naïve in the ways of politics and politicians, and lacking in the charisma needed to secure a mass following. Strangely enough, all this ultimately worked in his favour. Many of the leading politicians of the July Monarchy, such as Adolphe Thiers, had rapidly thrown in their lot with the new Republic, and they were now looking for a way of scrambling back into power. They lacked sufficient popular support to win power on their own; they therefore looked for somebody who could act as a figurehead and whom they were confident they would be able to manipulate once he was in power. Louis Napoleon was showing himself to be the ideal candidate. Thus, once the decision was taken to elect the President by a national vote with universal manhood suffrage, Louis Napoleon found himself being given the support of a large number of politicians and businessmen who thought they had found a puppet who would act as they instructed. As a result of this support Louis Napoleon's standing in political circles changed almost overnight from that of an idealistic and impractical adventurer to that of a credible candidate.

But Louis Napoleon was not elected merely because he had the cynical

support of some important people, useful as were their influence and
financial contributions. Many people voted for him because he claimed
to believe in policies of which they approved. A political observer at the
time wrote, 'Fundamentally, what France wants is not this or that form
of government, it is orderly and firm government'. It was this that Louis
Napoleon was offering the large section of the population that came to be
called the 'Party of Order', made up of those people whose main motivation was a fear of civil strife and the consequent threat to property,
trade and industry. The 'Party of Order' was not a political party. It had
no membership and no organization; it was merely a way of describing
the large group in society, including the Roman Catholic Church, who
preferred to keep things much as they were rather than to risk changing
them. Louis Napoleon's promise of strong government within a framework of a democratic Republic was much to their liking.

General Cavaignac, of course, had exactly the same appeal, and he
attracted many votes in the 'Party of Order'. But he could not compete
with the Bonaparte name and the emotional and sentimental associations
it had in so many minds. Nor could he portray himself as somebody who
would take a stand as a protector of the poor. He therefore attracted very
few votes in the towns whereas Louis Napoleon was projected in working
class areas as the man who could bring glory to France while ensuring
that the condition of the poor was improved.

Yet even without the weaknesses and disadvantages of his opponents,
the support of the politicians who hoped to manipulate him and policies
which could be presented so as to appeal to almost all sections of the
community, Louis Napoleon would have been in a very strong position
in a contest with more than eight million voters. The Bonaparte name
was important in the folk culture of the whole of France. It represented
hope to a population that needed to believe in a good future more than
anything else. Because of the multi-faceted nature of the Napoleonic
Legend, the Bonaporte name could spell out optimism for almost everybody no matter what future they hoped for. To the people of property it
meant security and effective government; to the Catholic Church it
meant sympathetic support and an end to Godless anti-clericalism; to the
socially aspiring it meant the opening of doors to people of wealth or
talent; to the nationalists it meant military victories and respect abroad;
and to the poor it meant the promise of better times ahead. It did not
matter that most of those who voted for the new Bonaparte had never
seen nor heard him, and that if they had they might not have been
impressed. They wanted to believe in him, and the propaganda put out
about him was such that they were given an excuse to believe and to vote
for him. This the people of France overwhelmingly did on 4 November
1848.

a) Louis Napoleon as President, 1848–52

The new Prince President, as he was called, was in no hurry to implement in detail the many promises he had made. Perhaps he realized that
for every decision he made he would create a sense of disappointment
somewhere for so many contradictory hopes of him were held. He was
safest building on his assets: his intense belief in himself and a devious
intelligence that could be used to win the loyalty of those who felt they
needed to be led. So he left politics and much everyday decision making
to the politicians and concentrated on building a more substantial power
base for himself. He paid ceremonial visits to most parts of the country
during which he conducted himself with such grace and charm that the
hundreds of thousands of people who saw him could not fail to be
impressed by the man they had chosen to be Head of State. He cultivated
the many leading figures in society whose desire was for strong
government irrespective of whether it was Empire, Monarchy, or
Republic. He built up a large group of dependents in important positions
who owed their place, their promotion, or their increased wealth to the
patronage of the President. As the months passed more and more official
posts were filled by men who owed a debt of personal loyalty to Louis
Napoleon.

At the same time the President's official actions and reactions to events
were all calculated to win the support of the people. A conscious decision
to positively disassociate himself from the Red Republicans was made for
they were seen to be the supporters of the politics of chaos and disorder.
The opportunity came in June 1849 when once again an attempt was
made to overthrow the Government by organizing an uprising in Paris,
but the Red Republican leaders had misjudged the mood of the people
and order was restored in a day. Louis Napoleon was able to show
himself as being firm and strong but not vindictively harsh.

This uprising had been partly aimed to demonstrate support for the
Republicans who had seized power in Rome and forced the Pope to flee.
However, it was clear to most observers that the Roman Republic would
eventually fall and that the Pope would be restored to his temporal
power. Louis Napoleon could either do nothing, in which case he might
lose the support of all the many French people who felt strongly about
the issue; intervene on the side of the Republicans, which would demonstrate his loyalty to the Republican form of government; or go to the aid
of the Pope, which would win the approbation of the many Catholics who
put their religion before their politics. The decision was made to show
resolution and hopefully to gain some military glory by sending an
expedition under General Oudinot to restore the Pope's authority in
Rome. Little military glory resulted, for the campaign was mishandled,
but Louis Napoleon was able to show that he was essentially a conservative rather than a revolutionary, news that was welcomed around Europe
as well as in the countryside of France.

This support of Catholic interests was also displayed in educational matters, which at the time were widely considered to be of central political importance, rather than being peripheral as is the case today. Many fervent Republicans were very hostile to the Catholic Church and the powerful influence it had on all aspects of life in France. They hoped to undermine the power of the Church by establishing a state system of compulsory education in which religion would have no part. The state schools would be staffed by lay people rather than by monks, nuns or priests. The Catholic authorities, on the other hand, wished to re-establish their hold on education which had been weakened by the 1830 Revolution and the politics of the July Monarchy, and looked for a return of the days when they were allowed to dictate what was taught in schools and universities and to veto the appointment of any teachers they thought unsuitable. The *Loi Falloux*, named after the minister who introduced it, was passed in 1850. It gave the Catholics much of what they wanted, for it encouraged the provision of Church schools to be staffed as the Church wished, made the teaching of religion compulsory in all schools, and did not establish a system of state education. Once again Louis Napoleon had shown himself a good friend to the conservative forces in society.

In the early months of his Presidency Louis Napoleon had been content to allow the politicians to think he was their puppet. The Constituent Assembly was replaced by a newly elected Legislative Assembly in May 1849 in which the 'Party of Order' held two-thirds of the 750 seats. It was therefore an easy matter for a ministry largely made up of politicians from the Orleanist regime and led by Odilon Barrot to secure continued parliamentary support. However, much to most people's surprise, the Barrot ministry was dismissed in October 1849, although its majority in the Assembly was secure, and a new ministry made up of the President's men was established. The process of consolidating power was continuing.

The major limiting factor to the progressive growth of Louis Napoleon's power was the Constitution, which debarred the immediate re-election of a President, and set May 1852 as the end of the Prince President's term of office. If Louis Napoleon was to have a political future, action had to be taken before then. The original hope was to secure a change in the Constitution so as to allow for a re-election, but an impressively organized campaign of public petitions failed to convince sufficient of the Legislative Assembly to produce the two-thirds majority needed to legalize such a change. Louis Napoleon therefore decided to implement what he claimed was the will of the people and change the Constitution himself.

His plans for a *coup d'état* were meticulously made and considering so many people were involved it was a major triumph that no more than rumours that something was about to happen leaked out. The date chosen was 2 December 1851, the anniversary of Napoleon I's coronation and also of his great victory at the Battle of Austerlitz. All went according to plan. The leading politicians who might have organized opposition to the coup were awoken and arrested at 6 o'clock in the morning; key public buildings were occupied by troops; the premises of opposition newspapers were taken over and publication halted; posters announcing the coup were printed overnight and were posted on to walls in all parts of Paris in the early morning; and large numbers of troops were brought into the capital in case of trouble. Some half-hearted attempts to raise barricades in the following days were violently repressed in an effort to convince people that opposition would not be tolerated, but generally there was no great hostility to the coup.

Later in the month a plebiscite was held in which the people of France were asked to approve the new arrangements, including a new parliamentary system and a ten-year period of office for the Prince President. Seven and a half million voted 'Yes'. This was more than 90 per cent of the electorate. Eleven months later another plebiscite was held to determine whether the people agreed to the Republic being turned into an Empire, with Louis Napoleon as Emperor. Again an overwhelming 'Yes' vote was recorded, and on 1 December 1852 the Second French Empire came into being, with the Emperor Napoleon III on the throne. The title Napoleon III showed a harking back to the first Empire and also emphasized the claim to legitimacy, for Napoleon's son was regarded as Napoleon II, although he had never ruled in France and had lived out most of his life in Austria.

b) Reasons for the Failure of the Second Republic

After less than five years the Republic had been brought to an end. In retrospect it is surprising that it had lasted so long. At the time, Republican forms of government were seen to have revolutionary overtones, suggesting social, economic and political turmoil, and rapid and radical change in the social system. It was for this reason that men of property and power throughout Europe regarded Republicanism as a public danger. Such was the case in much of France, although Republicanism received somewhat more support there because of a romantic attachment to the ideas of the First Republic that had grown up towards the end of Louis–Philippe's reign. But the Second Republic had been established by public acclaim in Paris. The people of France had not voted on the matter, and in the elections held in 1848 and 1849 only a minority of Republican Deputies had been returned. Had there not been a split between the Legitimists and the Orleanists in the Constituent Assembly, a Republican constitution would never have emerged. Thus the Republic had so few positive adherents that it was unlikely to survive any determined and well-organized attempt to overthrow it. General Cavaignac could have done so had he wished in the summer of 1848, the Orleanists might have done so at Christmas 1851 had their plans not been

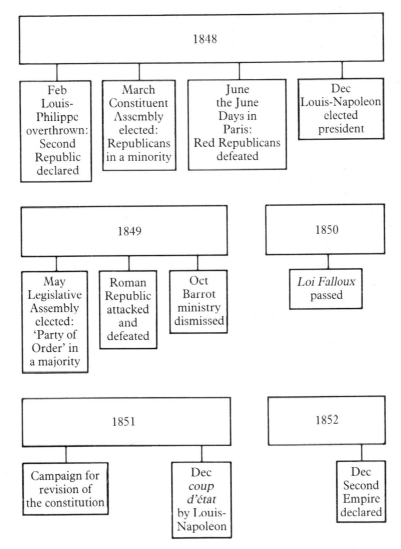

Summary – The Second Republic, 1848–52

forestalled by Louis Napoleon's own coup and the Bonapartists did do so once they judged the time to be right. The Second Republic failed to survive because few wished it to live once a reasonable alternative had been found. But this should not lead to an underrating of Louis Napoleon's achievement in gaining power so rapidly. He had worked hard, with determination and purpose, and had made skilful use of the advantages that fate and history had handed him.

Making notes on '*The Second Republic, 1848–52*'

Your notes on the Second Republic should allow you to remind yourself of what happened, when, and in what order. But the main purpose of the notes is to make you think and remember *why* things happened as they did. You are looking for causes, for reasons, for explanations. The following headings and sub-headings should help you to think about the right things:

1.   The Establishment of the Republic
1.1. What happend and why
1.2. Divisions among the Republicans
1.3. Pillars of Republican policy
        (Universal manhood suffrage; *le droit au travail*)
1.4. The Constituent Assembly, 1848–9
1.5. The June Days, 1848
1.6. The Constitution
2.   The Emergence of Louis Napoleon
2.1. The Presidential election, 1848
2.2. Louis Napoleon: the first forty years
2.3. Louis Napoleon: political views
2.4. Louis Napoleon: reasons for success in 1848
2.5. Louis Napoleon as President, 1848–52
        (building support; the *coup d'état*)
2.6. Reasons for the failure of the Second Republic

Answering essay questions on '*The Second Republic, 1848–52*'

You will at some stage be expected to use evidence from this chapter in helping to answer general questions on the period 1814–70. A discussion of these questions can be found on pages 130–131.

Very few essay questions concentrate exclusively on the years 1848–1852. Those that do, or are *largely* about this short period, tend to focus on two issues:

1. the rise of Louis Napoleon;
2. the replacement of the Second Republic by the Second Empire.
    Typical questions are:

    'Account for the success of Louis Napoleon in achieving the Presidency of the Second Republic and in establishing the Second Empire between 1848 and 1852.' (Cambridge, 1982)
    'Account for the growth of republicanism in France under Louis–Philippe and for the short life of the Second Republic.' (JMB, 1978)

Sometimes it is necessary to approach these two issues by considering them over a much longer time scale, as in:

'What features of French history in the years after 1815 help to explain the election of Louis Napoleon as President in 1848?' (London, 1979)

'What aspects of French history during the preceding thirty years help to explain the establishment of the Second Empire in 1852?' (London, 1978)

In all four questions you are asked to 'account for' or to 'explain'. In effect you are being asked 'what were the causes of . . . ?'.

In your work on Louis–Philippe you will have considered two ways of approaching causation questions – using the chronological device of long-term, short-term, and immediate causes, and organizing by topics such as political, economic, and social. You may have already decided that there is much to be gained by combining the two approaches to produce a table of causes laid out something like this:

	Long-term	Short-term	Immediate
Political			
Economic			
etc.			

Construct your own table of causes and use it to plan the paragraph headings of an answer to one of the four questions above. Choose your topic headings carefully to cover the aspects that are significant for the issues you are considering. You may find it easier to build up your topic headings as you think through a question. You should not be surprised if more than one of your boxes in the table remains empty. This is quite normal.

Source-based questions on 'The Second Republic, 1848–52'

1 Elections for the Constituent Assembly, March 1848
Read carefully Tocqueville's description of the situation in La Manche given on page 65 and answer the following questions:
a) Tocqueville claims that the attitude of the 'agricultural population' of La Manche towards the 1848 Revolution changed between late February and mid March. What was this change, and what was stated to be the major cause of it?
b) What can be learnt about Tocqueville's attitude towards the 1848 Revolution from this passage? Support your answer with as much evidence as possible.

2 The June Days, 1848

Read carefully Tocqueville's assessment of the June Days given on page 67 and answer the following questions:

a) In what two ways does Tocqueville claim the June Days were different from uprisings in Paris earlier in the century?

b) Tocqueville is hostile to the insurgents of the June Days. Write a paragraph of about 200 words setting out in neutral terms the arguments used by the insurgents to justify their actions.

3 The Constitution of 1848

Read carefully the Preamble to the 1848 Constitution given on page 69 and answer the following questions:

a) What is meant by 'III. It recognizes rights and duties older and higher than written laws'?

b) In what ways does the Preamble reflect the conservative nature of the majority of the Constituent Assembly? Support your answer with detailed evidence.

c) In what ways does the Preamble reflect a more liberal approach than existed under the July Monarchy? Support your answer with detailed evidence.

4 Louis Napoloen's views on party

Read carefully the extract from *Des Idées Napoléoniennes* given on page 73 and answer the following questions:

a) Louis Napoleon likens political activity to military activity. What implications does this have for the style of government he is advocating?

b) Why was Louis Napoleon hostile to the existence of political parties?

CHAPTER 5

The Second Empire, 1852–70: At Home

1 Politics

There has been much disagreement about the political stature of the man who rose from relative obscurity to become Emperor in little more than four years. Many historians have rated him very lowly, arguing that his faults far outnumbered his positive qualities. He has been described as an upstart adventurer who possessed some charisma and much animal cunning, but who was devoid of the intellectual ability to think through issues clearly, and of the steadfastness to follow a line of policy through to a conclusion. He has been characterized as an unprincipled ditherer. His reign has been seen as reaching a fitting climax in the disaster and disgrace of the Franco–Prussian War.

The tendency towards the virtual dismissal of Napoleon III as a serious political figure is most frequently found in general histories, especially ones that compare him with Bismarck. Perhaps it is not surprising that those historians who have chosen to concentrate their research on him have been more sympathetic. After all, there are not many students who choose to study in detail an historical character they consider to be of low standing. Thus most biographies and detailed studies of Louis Napoleon are at pains to stress his political successes and to distribute the blame for his failures as widely as possible. In particular, attention is drawn to the assertions that if Napoleon III had died in the early 1860s history's judgment of him would have been kinder, and that if the regime had not collapsed in 1870 it might have been seen as one of the rare examples of a political system that changed from virtual distatorship to parliamentary liberalism without major upheavals. But even his warmest admirers have found it impossible to claim that he was one of the leading political figures of the century. At best he can be regarded as a blend of rare qualities and fatal flaws.

Historians are not the only ones to disagree about Louis Napoleon the politician. Those who knew him well had very different views on the subject. The duc de Broglie, later to become the parliamentary leader of the Monarchists in the 1870s, found his opinion altering during 1851. He had seen him as being 'an adventurer who was both mad and incapable, with the confidence of a visionary in his imperial star, but lacking experience, knowledge or reliable resources of character and intelligence.' But the events of December 1851 forced him to question his former judgment.

1 What qualities did he possess which enabled him to achieve the very rare distinction of being still more popular after his trial period than beforehand? It was somewhat difficult to say, and our friends

in particular, knowing that he was devoid of those talents which
5 had made the fortune of public men under the parliamentary
régime – eloquence, administrative ability, wide knowledge and a
cultivated mind – were at a loss to understand. He had qualities of a
different order, patient skill, the art of not compromising himself
between the different parties which a fortuitous coalition had
10 grouped round him, the ability to dissimulate his thoughts, and
when on rare occasion he decided to speak in public, the gift of
finding the right word which reflected general opinion. In short
this madman, this "lout," as M. Thiers was fond of calling him,
without appearing to affect anybody, had made play with all those
15 who had laughed at him.

A fuller consideration of Louis Napoleon was undertaken by Alexis de
Tocqueville who had served under him as a minister while he was
President of the Second Republic. Tocqueville's views are particularly
interesting because they were written at the time and are therefore not
coloured by hindsight as many comments on Napoleon III have been. In
his pen portrait of the Emperor he writes:

1   As a private individual, Louis Napoleon possessed certain attractive qualities: an easy and kindly humour, a mind which was
gentle, and even tender, without being delicate, great confidence in
his intercourse, perfect simplicity, a certain personal modesty
5 amidst the immense pride derived from his origin. He was capable
of showing affection, and able to inspire it in those who approached
him. His conversation was brief and unsuggestive. He had not the
art of drawing others out or of establishing intimate relations with
them; nor any facility in expressing his views. He had the writer's
10 habit, and a certain amount of the author's self-love. His dissimulation, which was the deep dissimulation of a man who has spent his
life in plots, was assisted in a remarkable way by the immobility of
his features and his want of expression: for his eyes were dull and
opaque, like the thick glass used to light the cabins of ships, which
15 admits the light but cannot be seen through. Careless of danger, he
possessed a fine, cool courage in days of crisis; and at the same time
– a common thing enough – he was very vacillating in his plans. He
was often seen to change his direction, to advance, hesitate, draw
back, to his great detriment: for the nation had chosen him in order
20 to dare all things, and what is expected from him was audacity and
not prudence. It was said that he had always been greatly addicted
to pleasures, and not very delicate in his choice of them. This
passion for vulgar enjoyment and his taste for luxury had increased
still more with the facilities offered by his position. Each day he
25 wore out his energy in indulgence, and deadened and degraded
even his ambition. His intelligence was incoherent, confused, filled

with great but ill-assorted thoughts, which he borrowed now from
the examples of Napoleon, now from socialistic theories, sometimes from recollections of England, where he had lived: very
30 different, and often very contrary, sources. These he had laboriou-
sly collected in his solitary meditations, far removed from the
contact of men and facts, for he was naturally a dreamer and a
visionary. But when he was forced to emerge from these vague, vast
regions in order to confine his mind to the limits of a piece of
35 business, it showed itself to be capable of justice, sometimes of
subtlety and compassion, and even of a certain depth, but never
sure, and always prepared to place a grotesque idea by the side of a
correct one.

Generally, it was difficult to come into long and very close
40 contact with him without discovering a little vein of madness
running through his better sense, the sight of which always recalled
the escapades of his youth, and served to explain them.

It may be admitted, for that matter, that it was his madness
rather than his reason which, thanks to circumstances, caused his
45 success and his force: for the world is a strange theatre. There are
moments in it when the worst plays are those which succeed best. If
Louis Napoleon had been a wise man, or a man of genius, he would
never have become President of the Republic.

He trusted in his star; he firmly believed himself to be the
50 instrument of destiny and the necessary man. I have always
believed that he was really convinced of his right, and I doubt
whether Charles X was ever more infatuated with his legitimism
than he with his. Moreover, he was quite as incapable of alleging a
reason for his faith; for, although he had a sort of abstract adoration
55 for the people, he had very little taste for liberty. The characteristic
and fundamental feature of his mind in political matters was his
hatred of and contempt for assemblies. The rule of the Constitutional Monarchy seemed to him even more insupportable than that
of the Republic. His unlimited pride in the name he bore, which
60 willingly bowed before the nations, revolted at the idea of yielding
to the influence of a parliament.

Certainly it is clear that, whatever is the final balance of the judgment
of him as a man of politics, Louis Napoleon was a leader who was very
much out of the ordinary. His sense of mission was extremely strong. He
enjoyed power for its own sake, taking great pleasure from being the
centre of attention with companions around him whose main aim was to
fulfil his desires. But he was also genuinely motivated by a determination
to see a politically united and economically strong France restored to a
place of pre-eminence in the world. This was the driving force behind
most of his actions. This was the rationale for the political system he
developed.

* After the coup of 2 December 1851 and the plebiscite that followed it a new constitution was introduced. It came into effect on 14 January 1852. It was unashamedly authoritarian. Nearly all power was placed in the hands of the President, and nothing changed when the President became the Emperor at the end of the year, except that the term of office was extended from ten years to life. There was what appeared to be a parliamentary system but it was very different to what had gone before. Under Louis–Philippe the King had shared real power with the Legislative Assembly which had been able to bring down governments and force changes in policy. Under the constitution of 1852 the two Houses of Parliament, the Senate and the *Corps Législatif*, were purely consultative. They could initiate nothing of importance, they had no control over ministers, and when they voted they were merely deciding on what advice to give to the Head of State.

The impression that the Senate and the *Corps Législatif* were merely decorations used to dress up a dictatorship is strengthened when their composition and functions are studied in more detail. The Senate was made up of maximum of 150 people appointed directly by Louis Napoleon, to whom were added the Marshals of the army, the Admirals of the navy and the Cardinals of the Church, who sat as of right. The only duties of the Senate were to check to ensure that new laws were constitutional, and to announce changes in the constitution if they were requested to. The *Corps Législatif* was elected in 261 single-member constituencies by universal manhood suffrage for a period of up to six years. The Head of State could call elections more frequently if he so desired. Elections were totally free in theory, but in practice government officials – Prefects, Sub-Prefects, and Mayors – ensured that official candidates were well supported. So successful was this administrative support that in the first elections for the *Corps Législatif* in 1852, only eight declared opponents of the new regime were returned. The *Corps Législatif* played no part in drawing up legislation; it merely expressed an opinion, which could be ignored, on the draft laws that were presented to it by the Government. It met for only three months each year.

Yet it would be incorrect to suggest that the Senate and the *Corps Législatif* were totally under the control of Louis Napoleon. The Senators were appointed for life and could not be dismissed subsequently, even if they turned out to be hostile to the policies of the Government. The official candidates elected to the *Corps Législatif* were all prepared to offer general support to the regime, but only a minority felt any personal loyalty to Napoleon himself. It has been estimated that amongst those elected in 1852 more than 50 were ex-Legimists and ex-Orleanists, while there were only 70 who regarded themselves as Bonapartists. The majority were independent-minded notables (men of wealth and local social standing) who saw it as their duty to support the regime which offered the prospect of law and order in a restless world. They were prepared to co-operate while the Government's measures seemed to be in the interests of the country as they understood them, and while they were treated with the courtesy and respect they felt was their right, but they were in no sense slavish followers of the new Emperor.

The Senate and *Corps Législatif* were clearly not of prime importance in the new political system, although they were more than the rubber stamps they have sometimes been portrayed as being and needed to be managed with tact and understanding. More important was the *Conseil d'état*, made up of 40 members appointed by Louis Napoleon, and chaired by him until his elevation to Emperor made such an activity unsuitable. Even then he retained detailed control over the activities of the *Conseil d'état*, ensuring that it was presided over by somebody whose personal loyalty to him was beyond doubt. The *Conseil d'état* was responsible for drawing up the laws that were presented to the *Corps Législatif* for endorsement, and for discussing matters of government policy. The ministers of the Empire, appointed and dismissed as Napoleon wished, were members of the *Conseil d'état*, which carried out many of the duties of the British cabinet.

* This new constitutional system, which was so different from those that had immediately preceded it, was in fact almost identical to the system devised for the first Napoleon in 1800. The similarity was, of course, no accident. As Louis Napoleon himself explained:

1 I have taken as a model the political institutions which have, since the beginning of the century, and in similar circumstances, conso-lidated a society which had been upset and which raised France to a high degree of prosperity and greatness. I have taken as a model
5 since those institutions which, instead of disappearing with the first breath of popular unrest, had only been overthrown by a coalition of the whole of Europe against us. In a word, I said to myself: since, for fifty years, France has only gone on because of the administrative, judicial, religious and financial organization of the
10 Consulate and the Empire, why should we not also adopt the political institutions of the period?

Louis Napoleon genuinely believed that his mission was to complete the task begun by his uncle, and so it was natural to turn to the constitutional arrangements that had served France well during the Consulate and First Empire. These could then be developed subsequently along the lines that Napoleon I, while in exile on St Helena, had said he would have followed had he been given more time. Central to the Napoleonic vision of politics was an abhorrence of political parties, which were thought to encourage disunity, and were seen as getting in the way of good government. Thus, not only was no attempt made to build up a Bonapartist party after 1851, but the party which had been developed during Louis Napoleon's rise to power was allowed to wither. Instead, Napoleon attempted to utilize the talents of the 'best men' available, irrespective of their past politics. He did not demand that they agreed with him, or believed in him, before appointing them to posts of responsibility. He merely required an acceptance of his regime and a promise to work in the best interests of France.

This non-doctrinaire approach, copied directly from the time of the First Empire, was a great help in securing rapid acceptance for the new regime among the notables, the richest and most influential members of society. Nobody was automatically excluded from participation in the new system. Only those who chose to distance themselves from the new way of doing things were ruled out of consideration for positions of importance. Thus the coup of December 1851, and the declaration of the Empire in December 1852, did not result in massive changes in the people 'at the top'. Most of the politicians and admistrators who served the Emperor were men whose early careers had been in the service of previous regimes. A few of the personal followers of Louis Napoleon were appointed to powerful positions, but they were far outnumbered by the men who owed their importance to wealth and social standing rather than to any adherence to Bonapartism.

* Yet all was not sweet reasonableness from Louis Napoleon in the months following the coup. A conscious policy of harshness and toughness was adopted in order to give notice that violent opposition to the regime would not be tolerated. More than 26 000 arrests were made and over 10 000 men were either sent to Algeria or exiled from France. A strict system of press censorship was introduced which meant that adverse comment could not be widely spread. No newspaper was allowed to exist without the positive agreement of the Government. Those that did exist had to obtain a fresh agreement whenever there was a change in the staff they employed, and they had to deposit a large sum of money with the Government as surety of good behaviour. If the Minister of the Interior in Paris or a Prefect in the provinces felt that a newspaper was being critical of the Government a warning could be issued. After three such warnings a newspaper could be suspended with no trial and no right of appeal. Nor was opposition allowed to take the form of establishing political parties. Local groups were allowed to exist, but it was made illegal for them to join together in a national organization. Even the local groups, though, were not to remain uncontrolled. Every political meeting had to be attended by a government official.

Just as Napoleon attempted to discourage opposition, so he took active steps to encourage support. He realized the importance of creating strong bonds of loyalty between himself and the large, centralized, governmental machinery. This he did with great speed, doubling the salaries of Prefects and increasing the ability of government officials from the mayors of local communities upwards to 'reward' supporters of the regime with jobs and contracts. At the same time both the pay and the status of army officers were increased, and it was made clear to Church leaders that the regime would act in the interests of the Catholic authorities.

Within a few months the quarter of a million government officials, the armed services, and the Church were actively won over to support Louis Napoleon and the system he had created. The 'authoritarian Empire' was soundly established and enjoyed widespread support from all levels of society. Those opponents who were likely to stir up violent action against the regime were in prison or were abroad, while those who sought change by constitutional means would have found no widespread sympathy for their cause even if they had not been effectively muzzled by the press laws and by the restrictions placed on political activity.

It appeared that in the Second Empire France had at last found a political system that met its needs. The Emperor was powerful enough to provide strong leadership, he believed in the maintenance of law and order, while genuinely wishing to protect the interests of the underprivileged groups in the country. Advancement was open to all men of talent and ability who were prepared to work within the framework laid down by the Constitution, and all men would be involved in political life to the extent of voting in elections for the *Corps Législatif* and in the plebiscites that were held from time to time on major issues. Article 5 of the 1852 Constitution declared that 'The President is responsible to the French people'. This was no empty form of words. Louis Napoleon, both as Prince President until December 1852 and as Emperor afterwards, took his responsibility to the people of France seriously. He was therefore very open to the possibility of change if he could be persuaded that the change was in a direction desired by the majority of his subjects.

a) Changes in the Political System

Between 1860 and 1870 the political system of the Second Empire changed dramatically. The developments took place in three clearly defined stages. The first package of measures was announced in November 1860 and was implemented in the following year. For the first time the *Corps Législatif* was given the right to debate a statement of the Government's intentions and to receive a reply from ministers to the points of view expressed. This right was to be exercised once a year at the beginning of each session when the Emperor's address to the Assembly was read. In addition, an official report of the proceedings of the *Corps Législatif* was to be published, and newspapers were allowed to report the debates, as long as they did so in full. Edited extracts of debates were not allowed. The *Corps Législatif* was even given somewhat increased influence over the budget prepared by the Government. Instead of it being discussed and voted on in its entirety, it could now be debated section by section and detailed amendments could be suggested.

The changes of 1860–61 seem of so little significance, however, that some would argue that they are hardly worthy of mention. After all, nothing really changed as a result of them. The Emperor did not amend his policies as a result of the debate on his annual address; newspapers were not prepared to devote enough space to the happenings in the *Corps Législatif* to report them word for word; and any suggested changes in the budget could be ignored by the Emperor if he so wished. The power of the Head of State was still as absolute as it had previously been. Yet what happened in 1860–61 was seen by intelligent contemporary observers to be important. It was said that the symbolic significance of the changes far outweighed their practical effect, for they indicated that Napoleon III was serious in his intention to move towards a less dictatorial style of government as and when the time was right to do so. This interpretation was given more weight by the fact that it was common knowledge that his wife, the Empress Eugénie, who had a great influence on her husband, and all but one of his ministers were clearly opposed to the changes which the Emperor wished to introduce. If he was prepared to overcome such opposition, Napoleon III must have believed that what he was doing was important.

    * The second stage of political reform came in 1867–68. In January 1867 it was announced that in future the Senate and the *Corps Législatif* would be able to question a minister on the actions and policies of the Government as frequently as necessary. This right did not, of course, give the Assembly power over the Government's behaviour, but it did mean that it was impossible to hide from the public the mistakes made in official circles. This was especially so after 1868 when the press laws were so extensively relaxed that newspapers could come into being without needing to be approved by the Government, and when the laws controlling public meetings were virtually abandoned. From 1868 onwards Napoleon III's opponents were able to pour scorn on the regime in much the same way as had the opponents of Louis–Philippe in the mid 1840s. There can be no doubt that the confidence and credibility of the Second Empire were weakened by these attacks.

    * In 1869–70 came the political developments that resulted in the establishment of what has been described as the 'Liberal Empire'. In many ways this was a return to the type of parliamentary system of government that had existed under the July Monarchy. The Senate was turned into a proper upper house with the power to delay the passing of legislation. The *Corps Législatif* became a proper law-making body, able to initiate legislation, and not merely to comment on draft laws prepared by others. What is more, it was agreed that ministers should be responsible to the Assembly and should therefore command majority support in the two houses, to either of which they could not belong.

    To inaugurate these changes a new ministry was formed in January 1870, with Émile Ollivier as Prime Minister. Ollivier was a brilliant orator and shrewd politician, but his chief claim to fame was that he was a Republican, first elected to the *Corps Législatif* in 1857 as one of 'The Party of Five', the five Republicans who had managed to gain election in the face of opposition from official candidates. This was a dramatic development for although Ollivier had made it known for many years that he wished to work within the system to bring to fruition a truly parliamentary democracy, he was clearly committed to the aspiration of seeing the Empire eventually replaced by a Republic. For Napoleon III to join forces with such a man suggested that he was prepared to go a long way in seeking reconciliation with anybody who was willing to work within the framework of the law. In keeping with the spirit of these major changes it was decided to ask the French people for their agreement to what was in effect a new constitution. A plebiscite was duly held in May 1870 and almost as many people voted 'Yes' as had done so after Napoleon's coup of December 1851. It seemed that the Emperor had achieved what he had originally hoped for: a smooth transition to a form of government that kept the support of the people while sharing effective power very broadly.

It is tempting to see the liberalization of the Second Empire from a British perspective, imagining that Napoleon's intention was to establish a system such as that which was centred on the Houses of Parliament in Westminster. This would be a mistake, for there was in France no general belief that the best way to arrange matters was to give all power to the politicians, the elected representatives of the people. Much more there was a tradition of strong government, led by a powerful Head of State, whose actions were moderated by the people, directly through plebiscites, and indirectly through the work of elected representatives. Suspicion of politicians was if anything more widespread than suspicion of Kings or Emperors. It should therefore not be wondered at that the Constitution of 1870 left Napoleon with huge powers. It was still his right to appoint and dismiss ministers and he clearly meant to exercise it. It was also expected that the ministers would be putting forward the Emperor's policy, and it was accepted that if the Senate and *Corps Législatif* were unable to support this policy it was permissible for the Emperor to go over their heads and consult the people directly by holding a plebiscite. It is clear that in the France of 1870 this arrangement was widely accepted as representing the form of government that gave the best balance of authority and freedom, of strong leadership and participation. Had it not been for the coming of a disastrous war the Constitution of 1870 might have lasted for generations.

* When historians have written about the political changes of 1860–70 the central issue of concern has been why they happened. Were the developments part of a concerted attempt by Napoleon to convert his regime from a dictatorship into a liberal parliamentary system, or were the changes no more than an attempt by the Emperor to buy off increasing opposition and hence extend the life of his regime? Were the increased political rights granted as a favour from a position of strength, or were they concessions rung from a regime that was essentially weak?

The argument that Napoleon deserves no credit for the liberalization of the Empire, because he had no choice in the matter if he wished to survive, is a persuasive one. Leaving aside the changes of 1860–61, which in any case were relatively insignificant, it is possible to see the sharing of power running parallel with the growth of political opposition. Although the 1852 and 1857 elections for the *Corps Législatif* were well managed and successful from Napoleon's point of view, those of 1863 and, especially, 1869 were causes of considerable concern. In 1863, although only just over ten per cent of the seats went to opponents of the Emperor, a disturbing trend was evident. Of the 22 largest towns and cities in France, 18 including Paris, fell to the opposition. This suggested widespread urban discontent and raised fears of mob violence and revolution if something was not done to reduce the unrest. In 1869 things went from bad to worse. 43 per cent of the votes cast went against official candidates and 16 members were returned who were pledged to demand parliamentary forms of government. Many newspapers were equally clear in calling for changes in the system, and it is reasonable to see the coming of the 'Liberal Empire' as a direct result of an opposition that had forced the government on to the defensive.

Yet such an interpretation seems to spring from an assumption that dictators hang on to power at all costs and that democracy only comes about as a result of political struggle. It is not supported by close examination of the facts. A more accurate and balanced view is to argue that the political changes were brought about partly because Napoleon wished to move in this direction and partly because it seemed expedient to do so. It is true that the changes did generally follow expressions of widespread opposition to the existing situation, but this was because Napoleon needed some external pressure to help him overcome the opposition to reform that existed all around him in the Government. Besides Napoleon himself there was only ever one senior political figure who supported the cause of political reform. This was the Emperor's half-brother, the duc de Morny, who was the President of the *Corps Législatif* from 1854 until his death in 1865. It has been said that his death was the greatest disaster that befell the Second Empire, because he was a man of great ability and great political stature. His continued support of Napoleon would have made it possible for him to introduce the changes earlier and without giving the impression that they were belated concessions extracted from a weakening dictatorship.

Napoleon's ability to overcome the political inertia with which he was surrounded was markedly reduced after the duc de Morny's death. This was in part due to the fact that the Emperor could no longer find support in his immediate entourage for his policy of reform, and in part due to a dramatic decline in his state of health. In 1866 it was diagnosed that he was suffering from gallstones, for which there was no cure at the time. The result was that for much of the time he was in great pain, finding it hard enough to summon sufficient energy and will-power to complete his normal daily routine, let alone being able to drive forward unwilling ministers to implement reforming policies in which they did not believe.

A great stumbling block was Eugene Rouher who from 1866 was able to act as virtual Prime Minister, taking almost all day-to-day decisions as well as many longer term decisions, thanks to the physical frailty of the Emperor. So influential did Rouher become that he was nicknamed 'Le Vice-Empereur'. He was hostile to the idea of any reform. It was only after the election results of 1869 that Napoleon could summon sufficient resolve to sack Rouher and to implement a policy that he had been meaning to follow for some time. Thus while it is true to say that had it not been for the emergence of a strong opposition movement, reforms would not have come, it is not true to say that the changes came because of the growth of opposition alone. Napoleon clearly intended to move in a power-sharing direction, as the events of 1860–61 show; the emergence of the opposition largely provides an explanation of why the changes happened when they did. Thiers, in a letter to a friend, felt able to summarize Napoleon III's intentions.

1   . . . the Emperor followed partly his own inclinations and partly the way things pointed. His personal inclination has always been to think (he often used to tell me so) that repression was by nature temporary; he realized that sooner or later he would have to yield a
5   little to the re-awakening independence of opinion, and he found it gave him an appearance of great wisdom to forestall the day when concessions would no longer be voluntary. I think also his very strong affection for his son played its part in deciding him. Obviously he wanted to prepare the future for this child.

Even then it must be remembered that much of the opposition – at least that represented in the *Corps Législatif* – was dynastic opposition, that is opposition to the policies of the Government, rather than to the regime itself. There were plenty of Republicans in the large towns and cities, and there were some in the *Corps Législatif*, but the majority of those who called for a parliamentary stystem of government were happy to work within a Bonapartist Empire. Thus, even with memories of what happened to Louis–Philippe in 1848, there was never the pressure of 'reform or die'. Rather, Napoleon had an eye to the long-term survival of his regime and to the reign of his son, the Prince Imperial born in 1856, for he saw the strength of his Empire as being its ability to change and develop so as to conciliate the large majority of French people who had no doctrinaire views about the political system under which they wished to live.

2 Economic and Social Development

During his years of imprisonment in the fortress at Ham, Louis Napoleon had read and thought much about economic and social matters. The conclusions he had come to were neither original nor very profound, but they were broadly in keeping with the more advanced opinion of his day. The greatest impact on economic and social thinking in the early nineteenth century was made by the comte de Saint-Simon who had died in 1825. He had successfully convinced many contemporaries that the issue of the material prosperity of the common people was more important than the issues of freedom and equality, with which the French Revolution had mainly concerned itself. He argued that more would be done to improve the quality of life of ordinary people by removing them from poverty and material deprivation than by gaining for them the political rights enjoyed by the well-to-do. His followers, the Saint-Simonians, among whom Napoleon III might be numbered, saw progress very much in terms of creating additional wealth which would gradually percolate down through the layers of society until it eventually reached those at the bottom, those whose only capital was their own labour.

The key to creating this additional wealth was seen to be the availability of plentiful and cheap credit. With a steady supply of credit, entrepreneurs would be encouraged to begin new ventures, which in turn would provide more employment, which would increase the spending power of the country, which would increase the demand for the goods and services provided by the new ventures, and so more entrepreneurs would be encouraged to start more new ventures. To the Saint-Simonians it was almost as if they had discovered the secret of perpetual motion. If only they could find a government prepared to put their theories to the test the future would be assured and poverty would soon be a thing of the past.

* When Louis Napoleon came to power the banking system, such as it was in France, was in the hands of a few rich and conservative families. Foremost among these were the Rothchilds. The policy of these banking families was to lend money only where there was a high degree of security. They believed unsecured speculation to be irresponsible. Yet it was just this type of risk capital that the Saint-Simonians saw as being necessary. Louis Napoleon agreed with them, and realized that existing banks would not be prepared to change their approach to lending money. The answer had to be to establish new banks whose regulations would allow, and even encourage, them to provide entrepreneurs with the loans they needed. In 1852–53 three new banks came into being at the behest of the Government. It was clear from the start that the intention was to unlock the huge amount of capital that existed in France but that was not available to be borrowed by the creators of new wealth.

The most important of the new banks, founded in 1852, was the *Crédit Mobilier*. This was run by the two Péreire brothers, close associates of Louis Napoleon, who in many ways typified the Second Empire. They drew their support not from the privileged few, but from the masses, being the first bank to welcome the savings of the hundreds of thousands of ordinary people who were largely despised by the very rich.

The bank's methods were unorthodox and brash, and it conducted its affairs with a flair for publicity which rapidly turned the dislike felt by long-established banking houses into hatred as the realization dawned that the new system was a major challenge, rather than being the minor irritant it had at first appeared. Public confidence in the *Crédit Mobilier* was based on the belief that the aura of infallibility that surrounded the Péreire brothers was genuine, and that their Saint-Simonian claims were correct. Of course, it also helped that the bankers were known to be special favourites of the Emperor. With hindsight it is possible to see that the *Crédit Mobilier* bubble would continue to grow as long as conditions were right for economic expansion, but that it would probably burst once a period of prolonged recession came. Its opponents were to have the last laugh, and were able to claim that their description of it as 'the biggest gambling house in the world' was based on more than envy and spite (see page 101).

* For much of the life of the Second Empire, however, the new banks provided the capital of many of the spectacular projects which took place in France and which gave the impression of rapid economic advancement. Most noticeable to native and visitor alike was the growth of a large railway network, linking regions of France in a way that was totally new. In Britain it had been the opening of the Liverpool to Manchester railway in 1830 that had started the rush to build new lines; in France a much more cautious 'wait and see' approach had been adopted towards this revolutionary form of transport. After all, large sums of money were still being spent on building canals and opening rivers to commercal navigation. If railways were a success most of this money would have been wasted. Under Louis–Philippe no strong lead had been given by the Government, and although over 1700 kilometres of track had been laid down there had been no 'grand design'. The result was a series of largely unconnected railways linking pairs of towns between which there was likely to be enough traffic to justify the expenditure required to build a railway. Louis Napoleon, along with many others, saw the need to create a railway system which would link the regions of France together, making it possible to move people and goods from one part of the country to another at speed, cheaply and in safety. There is some evidence that he was aware of the desirability of being able to move armies with a rapidity undreamt of by his uncle, but this was not his main motive in giving active support to the railway lobby. It was more that he was attracted by the general, and largely unexplored, possibilities that the new technology provided. A new network of communications criss-crossing the map of France, almost as an end in itself, was enough to capture the imagination of the Emperor.

More was done in the France of the Second Empire than was done in Britain to smooth the path of the speculative railway builder. Regulations were designed so as to encourage co-operative ventures that served the public interests rather than supporting those whose only desire was quick profit. The Government guaranteed a minimum rate of interest to be paid on the shares of railway companies specially to help those who were prepared to build parts of the network which served areas of relatively sparce population and which therefore offered the prospect of only modest financial returns. This meant that investors, be they banks or private individuals, were not only assured against the loss of money lent to a railway company; they were also sure that they would receive at least a small annual return on their capital. It is impossible to quantify the effect of this positive support from the Government, but it must have done something to convince the people of France that investment in railways provided exciting possibilities of high returns on capital. Certainly the atmosphere was right for the increased pace of railway building that took place during the Second Empire, and for an acceptance of the principle that railways were a public utility, the provision of which the Government should both encourage and regulate. By 1870 the 1770 kilometres of railway that had existed in 1848 had grown tenfold, to reach a figure of nearly 17 700 kilometres. France now possessed a railway network that was not significantly inferior to that which had been built in Britain, despite her slower start.

* Apart from the building of railways, the development that made the greatest visual impact on France during the Second Empire was the huge programme of urban renewal that was undertaken. As a result, the centres of most major towns and cities were greatly changed, often beyond recognition. The tangle of essentially medieval streets was replaced by a series of spacious boulevards and squares built to an overall plan. In many towns the rebuilding only affected a very small area, but in France's three major cities, Paris, Lyons, and Marseilles, the redevelopment was on a scale not to be tackled in any other part of the world until the mass destruction of war in 1939–45 made similarly ambitious projects a necessity. In Paris in particular, a conscious effort was made to create a capital that was in keeping with the new Napoleonic age. Order and grandeur were the keynotes of the plan for the new city which Napoleon III himself played an active part in drawing up and monitoring. The detailed work was entrusted to Baron Haussmann. He was appointed Prefect of the Paris region in 1853, a post which he held for 17 years. Because of his great energy and enthusiasm he was able to overcome the many objectors who found that the overall plan made it necessary to destroy their homes or their businesses, forcing them to move to a less convenient location. Nothing was allowed to stand in the way of what was intended. In this the rebuilding of Paris was a typical example of the style of strong government that is common in dictatorships.

The central idea in the remodelling of the capital was that there should be a series of long, straight and broad roads radiating from a central square, with a large number of interconnecting roads and squares to complete the pattern. The buildings lining these roads were to be of a pre-planned elevation, and in an architectural pattern that was pre-scribed by the authorities. Most of these buildings were to be used as shops, offices, or residences for the well-to-do. A remarkable total of 136 kilometres of new streets were designed and built in this way, and the Paris of the modern tourist is largely the city rebuilt under the supervision of Haussmann. By any standards this was a remarkable achievement, which added greatly to the prestige of the regime, as well as providing a huge amount of employment for the urban working classes.

Yet the work of Haussmann, actively supported by the Emperor, has had more than its fair share of critics, both at the time and subsequently. Contemporary opponents of Haussmann concentrated on his high and mighty attitude which was shown both by the way in which he refused to amend his plans however strong were the arguments against him, and by the highly unorthodox means he used to raise money for his venture, some of which would have landed a private individual in prison.

Later critics have made much of both the limitations of Haussmann's scheme and the unhelpful consequences of some of his actions. It is noticeable that the new Paris was often only one street deep, for behind many of the new boulevards were the remains of the old city – overcrowded, insanitary and dilapidated. What is more, the much vaunted new sewers were only designed to take rainwater; 'night soil' still had to be carted away as it always had been. These shortcomings give credence to the claim that Haussmann, and Napoleon, were only interested in appearances, rather than caring about the conditions in which the poor lived.

It seems that self-glorification was a major motive behind the rebuilding of Paris, although the claim that Napoleon was sweeping away the areas that were ideal for the erection of barricades at times of revolution and replacing them with broad, straight streets down which canon could be fired with ease, should not be taken too seriously. But the claim that scant attention was paid to the needs of the poor in Paris is substantiated when one considers the major side effect of Haussmann's policy. Many of the buildings swept away were those in which manual workers and their families rented rooms. In their places were built premises for commerce and homes for the rich. Thus the displaced workers and their families were forced to seek accommodation further afield, and just at a time when the sorts of rooms they could afford were much in demand as thousands of labourers were attracted to Paris in the hope of obtaining work in either demolition or rebuilding. If the planners had really cared about the conditions endured by the poor some effort would have been made to provide modern homes for the labouring poor, perhaps along the lines of those advocated by Prince Albert in Britain at the time.

* Not all the additional credit made available through the new banks was used to build the railway network or to rebuild the centres of major cities: a considerable proportion of it was invested in overseas ventures. The most famous of these was the building of the Suez Canal, which was

engineered by a Frenchman and financed by French capital. Started in 1859, it was completed ten years later, just in time for its opening to be yet another well managed set-piece to publicize the energy and initiative of the Second Empire. Less dramatic, although with implications for the future, was the financing of railway building in Russia, which thus became a part of France's sphere of economic influence in much the same way as did Spain and Italy, and as did the Americas and much of the Far East for Britain.

* What may seem surprising is the fact that a relatively small proportion of the new credit was invested directly in either agriculture or industry. In part this was because the concepts of industrialization and increased productivity were not greatly valued by any of the powerful groups in the France of the time. If anything, industrialization was seen as a necessary evil for those countries facing a rapid increase in population and the consequent need to find employment for an ever growing number of 'hands', but this was not the situation in France where the population was rising very slowly. It increased by only some three per cent during the period of the Second Empire. Whereas in Britain enthusiasm for agricultural improvement and resulting increased productivity had been apparent throughout the century, in France the landowners, who were overwhelmingly peasant smallholders, saw little merit in investing in land they already owned. The widely held view was that if there was money to be spent, it should be used to increase the size, not the quality, of the holding. Given these values and attitudes on the part of the governing classes and of the landowning majority, it is not so surprising that agriculture and industry made relatively little use of the new sources of finance.

This is not to say that little was invested in industry during the Second Empire. It was just that the huge majority of industrial firms in France were family concerns, employing relatively few workers, and little in need of injections of credit from outside. The tradition was that profits provided the source of fresh investment, and it was a custom that most industrialists wished to continue. The financial advantages of being in debt to others were not readily apparent in a world of low inflation, and the morality of family finances was still widely accepted in the business world. If to be in debt was not quite a sin, it was very near to being so.

The statistics for industrial growth during the Second Empire are open to all sorts of interpretations, depending on what one wishes to prove. Some historians have seen the period as one of major industrial growth, but it seems that this view is hard to maintain if a wide range of industries is investigated. It is true that the iron and steel industries benefited from new inventions as well as from the great increase in demand created by the railway boom, but across the industrial sector as a whole annual growth was not out of step with that recorded for the reign of Louis–Philippe or the early years of the Third Republic. Although the Second Empire did see some industrial success stories, there was no general leap forward, such as that which was taking place in Britain, Belgium or Germany. Even if there had been, it would not have been the result of action by Napoleon, for he clearly did not see the political and military importance of a rapidly expanding industrial base in the way that Bismarck claims to have done. As a Saint-Simonian, Napoleon was much more interested in unlocking existing wealth in the form of cheap credit, than in creating new wealth through large-scale industrialization.

So the France of 1870 was structurally very similar to the France of 1848. The large majority of the people lived in the countryside and earned their living from the land. There had been some drift to the towns, meaning that nearly a third of the population was now urban, compared with the quarter in 1848, but relatively few of the new townspeople were living in new industrial areas, of which France had few. Instead, the trend was for the existing towns with their industries based on small workshops to attract those who left the land. Large factories were few and far between, and the percentage of the population engaged in industrial activity of any kind had only risen to 6.5. In fact it could be argued that on balance Napoleon did more to inhibit French industry than he did to encourage it. Certainly that was the view held by many of his opponents in the years after 1860.

* Like most politicians Napoleon was a great borrower of other people's ideas. This, in itself, should not lay him open to criticism, for given the wide-ranging activities with which most political leaders must concern themselves it is almost inescapable. The pity was that Napoleon did not always show very good judgment in choosing which ideas to adopt. While he had been sheltering in Britain after his escape from Ham the great debate on Free Trade, especially in relation to the Corn Laws, had been taking place. Napoleon became convinced that Free Trade was the goal to be worked towards for all countries in all parts of the world. It can be readily understood why for Britain the dismantling of the massive structure of complex customs duties that existed in most countries was an attractive proposition. Her industrial revolution had left her with a clear lead in the key textile, iron and steel, and metal products industries, where in terms of price, quality, and output there was little competition. In this situation it made sense to work towards a pattern of freer trade in which less economically advanced countries would be able to sell their raw materials to Britain and use the income gained in this way to buy British manufactured goods. Many people in Britain supported the cause of Free Trade largely for the selfish reason that it was likely to increase the country's economic domination of the world. In France the same situation did not prevail. French industry was growing and developing, but depended more on a large and secure home market than on selling abroad. Most French industrialists saw the possibility of Free Trade as a threat to this home market, which was currently effectively protected from foreign penetration by high customs duties.

Napoleon was not stupid. If the only argument in favour of Freer

Trade had been the one that won so much support in Britain, he would have seen that it was in France's best interests to maintain protection. But the movement towards Free Trade had taken on the form of a moral crusade, holding out the prospect of a golden age of interdependence in which every country would produce those products for which it was most fitted, with free trade ensuring that goods could move readily from place to place and the end result being the abolition of all forms of material deprivation. In the same way as the Saint-Simonians offered a complete answer to the economic problems of the past, so did the Free Traders. It was the simplicity and coherence of the Free Trade case that appealed to Napoleon and allowed him to think of himself as the wise father of his people, arranging things so that a prosperous future would be assured.

The Emperor's Free Trade vision was shared by very few people in France and was vehemently opposed by nearly all the leading figures in manufacturing industry, who greatly feared competition from British firms if they were to be allowed into France on equal terms. Yet Napoleon was not prepared to give way, despite the fact that his early efforts to move towards Free Trade stirred up so much opposition that he was forced to withdraw his plans and find a way of bringing about changes that depended on his authority alone. The answer was not to bring in a new law, which needed to be dealt with by the *Corps Législatif*, but to make treaties with other countries, for the power to do so was the Emperor's alone. Thus, between 1860 and 1865, nine trade treaties were signed between France and other European countries. The first and most important treaty was that signed with Britain. From the British side much of the negotiation was done by Richard Cobden, one of the leaders of the Anti-Corn-Law League whose success in 1846 in obtaining the repeal of the Corn Laws had created such an impression on the exiled Louis Napoleon. It was probably this personal connection that made the Cobden Treaty of 1860 possible, for it was rightly hailed in Britain as something of a coup. The traditionally prohibitively high tariffs in France were to be gradually lowered until they virtually disappeared. In return the duties on French goods, except wines and spirits, entering Britain were removed.

It is somewhat ironic that despite the high hopes and great fears that were associated with Free Trade, historians have not been able to identify any consequences of great significance. Certainly French industry was not destroyed, although some firms using antiquated methods did go out of business, supposedly because of foreign competition. There is even some evidence that French industry benefited from the increase in economic activity that followed the lowering of tariff barriers. On balance, it is probable that the freeing of trade brought about on Napoleon's insistence resulted in a slight increase in prosperity in France, without doing great damage of the type that opponents envisaged. But the position is not clear, and possibly never will be, for it is impossible to estimate what would have happened had the trade treaties never been signed.

a) Significance of the Developments

Generally, the economic and social policies of the Second Empire have not found favour with historians, and they certainly met with increasing critiscism at the time. The feeling is very much one of disappointment. In the late 1840s and early 1850s there were such high expectations of the new Bonaparte, for he seemed to be genuinely concerned about the welfare of ordinary people and to be decisive and powerful enough to ensure that something would happen. Yet the results were not impressive. Much noise was made about the show pieces of the regime – the new approach to credit, the rebuilding of the cities, railways and free trade – but the reality of what happened did not match up to the promises that had been made.

Perhaps a symbol of the sourness that became widespread in the later 1860s was the collapse of the *Crédit Mobilier* and the Péreire brothers in 1867. Although the approach to risk capital adopted by the brothers was likely to lead to severe problems in a time of recession, such as that brought about by the dislocation of international trade caused by the American Civil War between 1861 and 1865, there is no reason why these should have been disastrous. The total destruction of the bank, and the consequent loss to hundreds of thousands of small investors, was brought about because the orthodox bankers, such as the Rothschilds, did all in their power to make it happen. In this way they could seriously discredit a financial system and a regime that they believed to be founded at best on irresponsibility and at worst on a confidence trick. At the same time Haussmann ran into real difficulties in the continued financing of his rebuilding of Paris and there were more public scandals surrounding his unorthodox methods.

Thus the lasting achievements of the Empire in social and economic affairs are less substantial than seemed likely in 1852, when Louis Napoleon brought the Second Republic to a close. Paris was more beautiful and transport was much improved, but for the ordinary people life went on much as before. The 1860s did see the granting of the right to form trade unions and the right to strike, but these were poor substitutes for the general care of the people that had been promised. It is therefore small wonder that radical republicanism, which was slow to recover from the June Days of 1848, should become an increasingly strong force in the large towns and cities, as the election results of 1863 and 1869 showed. By 1870 Napoleon was increasingly unpopular among the traditional upper class who were tired of his championing of the *nouveaux riches;* among the industrialists who were still not reconciled to the moves towards Free Trade; and among the urban poor who no longer had faith that their interests would be protected. Yet it was a failure of foreign policy that was to lead to the end of the Bonapartist dream, for although

failures in domestic policy had removed much of the basis of support for
the regime, there needed to be a dramatic happening to bring about the
changes that most people now regarded to be in the long term interests of
France.

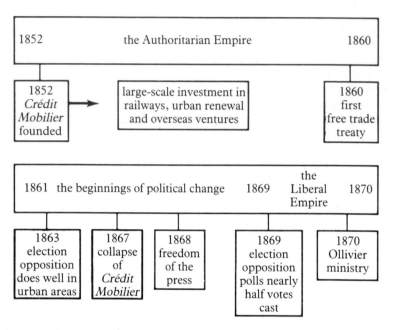

Summary – The Second Empire, 1852–70: At Home

Making notes on *'The Second Empire, 1852–70: At Home'*

The notes you make on 'The Second Empire: At Home' are likely to
concentrate on the answers to three questions: 'What happened?',
'Why?', and 'With what effects?'. It is advisable to ask all three questions
of each topic dealt with in this chapter. At the same time it would be
sensible to watch out for points that could be used in making an assessment of Napoleon III and the role he played in the history of France,
1852–70.

The following headings and sub-headings provide a workable
framework:

Source-based questions on 'The Second Empire, 1852–70: At Home'

1 The Character of Louis Napoleon

Read carefully Broglie's and Tocqueville's assessments of Louis Napoleon given on pages 83–85, and answer the following questions:

a) The extracts from Broglie's assessment of Louis Napoleon suggest that many politicians misjudged him to begin with. What were the major causes of this misjudgment? Support your answer with evidence.

b) Of which aspects of Louis Napoleon's character and behaviour is Tocqueville openly critical?

c) Is Tocqueville more in agreement with Broglie's initial assessment or with his revised assessment? Support your answer with detailed evidence.

d) Using only evidence from the extracts, write a paragraph of about 200 words explaining what the key aspects of Louis Napoleon's political character were.

2 The Constitution of 1852

Read carefully Louis Napoleon's explanation of his reasons for basing the 1852 Constitution on that of the Consulate given on page 87, and answer the following questions:

a) What three reasons does Louis Napoleon give for basing the 1852 Constitution on that of 1800?

b) It would be reasonable to suggest that Louis Napoleon's statement was made for propaganda purposes rather than in order to give a genuine account of his motives. What evidence is there in the extract to support this view?

3 Napoleon III's motives in liberalizing his regime
Read carefully the extract of the letter from Adolphe Thiers given on page 93, and answer the following questions:
a)   What does Thiers suggest were Napoleon III's motives in liberalizing his regime before he was forced to?
b)   What are the strengths and weaknesses of the extract as evidence about Napoleon III's motives for acting as he did?

CHAPTER 6

The Second Empire 1852–70: Abroad

1 The Approach to Foreign Affairs

Napoleon I's fame rests largely on his remarkable military exploits and on the huge empire he built for France as a result of them. Nobody since the great Charlemagne, a thousand years before, had managed to establish such dominance over continental Europe, and rarely had France's international status been so high. When the nephew of the great General became President of the Republic in 1848 and Emperor in 1852, both the people of France and the governments of Europe felt that the period of France's international subservience which began in 1815 was at an end.

Louis Napoleon thought so too, although he had sufficient insight to realize that he must proceed with caution. Just as Louis–Philippe had been very aware that a bellicose policy in 1830 on behalf of the Belgian rebels would probably have resulted in the Eastern Powers of Russia, Austria, and Prussia intervening in France to restore the Bourbons, Louis Napoleon knew that once the revolutions of 1848–9 in central Europe had been suppressed, little provocation would be needed to encourage the Powers to bring the Second Republic to an end. He also gauged the mood of the French people accurately, for he was aware that although there was a nostalgic harking back to the years of greatness, few wished to pay the price of war and dislocation that would be necessary if France were once again to challenge Europe. He therefore summed up his policy in the somewhat surprising catch-phrase, '*l'Empire, c'est la paix*' (the Empire is peace).

However, it would be misleading to suggest that Louis Napoleon intended to abandon war totally as an instrument of foreign policy. Rather, he hoped that it would be possible to restore France to her traditional place as the leading European Power without the need to resort to a long and major war. Certainly he had no intention of accepting the inferior position for France that the country had occupied under Louis–Philippe. Yet the catch-phrase was more than a cynical attempt to allay the fears of those, at home and abroad, who believed that his assumption of virtually dictorial powers would be a prelude to international turmoil and anarchy. Louis Napoleon genuinely wished to avoid war if possible, although he was prepared to countenance a small-scale military enterprise if he could not attain his objectives in other ways. But the other, diplomatic, ways were normally pursued with vigour and right up to a declaration of war, as in 1859 and 1870. Even then Napoleon hoped that a swift peace could be made. He certainly was no warmonger.

* In foreign policy, as in domestic policy, Napoleon was attracted to a small number of key ideas which he attempted to follow through as his policy developed. One of these was that if France was to be once again a major force in international affairs, it would be necessary to destroy the territorial settlement made at Vienna in 1815, as this was a continuing symbol of France's defeat at the hands of the other Powers. He was tempted to support any move which was against the spirit or the letter of the Vienna Settlement, espeically if it was likely to weaken the united front of the three Eastern Powers which still seemed to be working together to prevent any growth in France's power or influence.

* One of the forces likely to lead to the disintegration of the Vienna Settlement was nationalism. Napoleon I had seen nationalism as holding the key to much of Europe's future, and his nephew readily accepted this analysis, for it had the advantage of offering the prospect of discomfiting the established powers of Europe as well as being a part of the Bonapartist tradition. Russia, Austria and Prussia occupied the whole of Poland between them, while Austria and Prussia vied for dominance among the German states and Austria was in control of most of northern Italy. If Napoleon III could stir up trouble among nationalistically minded Poles, Germans or Italians, there was a realistic prospect of France gaining at least a negative advantage in that she had nothing to lose while others did.

* Napoleon III was a proud man who took seriously both the honour of his family and of his country. He was extremely sensitive about how he and his country were treated by others and was quick to take offence if he suspected that a slight had been intended. Equally, he was greatly attracted to the trappings of international prestige and status and was as satisfied by the glory of being treated as important and successful as he was by the substance of international power and influence. Appearances mattered to him almost more than reality. This pursuit of glory – *la gloire* – going alongside a desire not to have to resort to war, led Napoleon III into some very strange and otherwise inexplicable situations, especially in his dealings with Bismarck, which many historians have interpreted as proving that he was muddle-headed and relatively unintelligent. Certainly it can be said that elements of his approach to foreign affairs were contradictory. Consequently he sometimes found himself in situations where he was tempted to go in both directions at the same time and so appeared to be confused and indecisive. It seems that never did he properly establish a set of priorities for the conduct of his foreign policy.

* Throughout Napoleon III's reign the statesmen of the other European Powers retained the suspicion that at the heart of French foreign policy lay a desire to extend her territorial boundaries. This was not surprising as for centuries French leaders had sought to make a reality of the concept of 'natural frontiers'. It was reasonable to assume that nothing had changed, especially as the Vienna Settlement had reversed the gains made under Napoleon I.

To a large extent, of course, France had long ago reached her 'natural frontiers' – of the Channel and the Atlantic in the West, of the Pyrenees in the South-West, of the Mediterranean in the South, and of the Alps in much of the East – but two contentious areas remained. In the North the only 'natural frontier' that could realistically be aspired to was the River

Rhine, but to reach the Rhine France would not only have to take over the French-speaking areas of Belgium and Luxemburg, but would also need to gain control of extensive areas peopled by Dutch and German speakers. In the south-east, a mixture of historical factors had resulted in a significant area of land to the west of the highest peaks (Savoy and the county of Nice) being regarded as a part of 'Italy'. Not only were there numbers of Italian speakers living there, but the ruling family of Piedmont had for centuries been the rulers of Savoy. It could be said that France had a geographical claim to this land.

Strangely enough, Napoleon III seems not to have been strongly motivated by a desire to acquire more land for his country. He was much more interested in prestige and international standing than he was in territorial expansion, When he did make moves to extend France's boundaries it was largely because his sense of pride demanded that if another country was gaining something, France must receive a 'bribe' for allowing or helping it to happen. In the 1850s and 1860s interest in colonial expansion was generally at a low-ebb in all countries. The fact that during the Second Empire France gained additional territory, especially in Senegal in West Africa and in Indo-China, was the result more of chance and the initiative of local officials than of any centrally directed policy. The Emperor was pleased to feel that an increase in the Empire overseas was a reflection of his own growing power and prestige, but he made no attempt to acquire territory as an end in itself.

* For the sake of clarity and convenience, historians tend to deal with domestic and foreign affairs separately. In the mind of Napoleon III, of course, there was no such separation. Sense can only be made of the foreign policy of the Second Empire if it is recognized that Napoleon's actions abroad were in part the result of his wish to win or keep the support of important sections of the French population. In the first ten years of power he was particularly keen to be supported by the Catholic Church which was gaining an increasing hold on the minds of both the intellectual élite of the nation and the broad mass of the people in the countryside. The widespread anti-clericalism of the late eighteenth and early nineteenth centuries was becoming less fashionable. This desire to champion the Catholic cause never completely disappeared but it became harder and harder to sustain once the Pope declared himself to be opposed to modern 'errors' such as nationalism, for Napoleon was not prepared to renounce what was one of the emotional corner stones of his approach to foreign affairs. Towards the end of his reign, however, he became more and more concerned to give the people what they wanted. In deciding the stance he would take in international disputes he was increasingly swayed by public opinion as it was relayed to him from government officials throughout the country.

2 Succccesses

a) The Crimean War

The Crimean War of 1854–6 does seem to be one of the most nonsensical wars of modern times, both in the events that led up to it and in the way it was fought. It was the first major international dispute in which Napoleon was involved after his seizure of power in December 1851. His inexperience showed, for, throughout the affair, he was reacting to events rather than initiating them himself.

Unfortunately, nobody was able to take a firm grip of the situation, and what should have been solved diplomatically was allowed to drift into war. Napoleon's intentions during the 12 months that led up to the declaration of war in March 1854 were never clear. He had a notion that by forcing Turkey to accept France as the protector of Catholics within the Turkish Empire and by pressing the claim of the Catholics rather than monks of the Greek Orthodox Church to have control of the Holy Places in Palestine, he was both enhancing France's prestige and assuring himself of the continued support of the Church in France. But he seems to have had no idea how matters could be resolved so that the major participants – France, Russia, Turkey, and subsequently Britain – could agree terms without there being an unacceptable loss of face by anyone.

In the event, both France and Russia publicly stated their determination to be the major influence on the Sultan of Turkey in such a way that it was virtually impossible for either to compromise without appearing to be defeated. Once the Sultan saw how heavily committed the French were, he was able to provoke Russia into military action because he knew that France, and probably Britain, would come to his assistance as they could not afford to see a Russian victory. Thus Napoleon was manipulated by the Turks who had seen a way of ridding themselves of the Russian threat which had been hanging over them for 25 years. France did not want a war, but by the Spring of 1854 it seemed the only alternative to accepting Russian dominance in Turkey.

'*L'Empire, c'est la paix*' seemed to lack conviction when within 18 months of saying it, Napoleon III found himself engaged in a war with one of the Great Powers. Yet there were mitigating circumstances if it is understood what Napoleon really meant by his policy of seeking peace. He did, after all, attempt to find diplomatic solutions to the problem and only opted for war when it was clear that he must either fight or be humiliated. Nor was he entering on a 'proper' war of the type that had traditionally meant a struggle in the heartland of Europe, especially along the Rhine or in Northern Italy. The war against Russia was to be fought a long way from France in a part of the world that did not really count. Given the values and attitudes of the time an overseas war, such as the Crimean War or the one that had been fought in Algeria since 1830, was merely an expedition, not thought to be significant when compared with the major European struggles that France had been engaged in from time to time for two hundred years.

This is not to argue, however, that Napoleon III's actions in the year leading up to the outbreak of the Crimean War showed consistency or a clear sense of purpose, for they did not. Yet there was, throughout, the feeling that there was a major advantage to be gained for France whatever happened. If the Russians voluntarily yielded their pre-eminent position of influence with the Sultan in Constantinople and accepted the French on at least equal terms, Napoleon would have gained greatly in international standing. If, on the other hand, Russia remained intransigent and failed to make even reasonable concessions, it was likely that the united front of the Quadruple Alliance powers – Russia, Austria, Prussia, and Britain – which had imposed the Vienna Settlement on France would be shattered. As it turned out, the strategy succeeded almost beyond Napoleon's expectations. While Russia was an enemy, Britain was an ally, and Austria and Prussia were at least benevolently neutral, much to Russia's chagrin. The united front of France's potential enemies had been destroyed.

Despite his dislike of war, it was perhaps only to be expected that the nephew of France's greatest ever military commander would be tempted to try out the army and navy of which he was now in total command. If he was a little like a small boy with a new toy, he was not being as irresponsible as he would have been if he had lived in the age of total war or nuclear weapons. In 1854 warfare was still generally viewed as a kind of sport in which the personal qualities of courage, steadfastness and loyalty could be put to the test. Few people considered it immoral to use small-scale warfare as an extension of normal diplomacy.

* Yet the war that actually developed was a great disappointment to all concerned. Not only did it fail to arouse much enthusiasm in France, but it also failed to be the short, sharp shock that had been intended. The seige of the naval base of Sebastopol in the Crimea by British and French forces took much longer than expected and it was not until September 1855 that the town fell. In the meantime reports from the Crimea had been full of tales of inefficiency and mismanagement. It is true that it was the British who were by far the most disorganized of the allies and that the Russians were barely better, but this hardly represented *la gloire* which Napoleon had sought, even if the campaign was not the disgrace for France that it was for the two other major Powers.

* After Sebastopol had fallen there seemed little point in fighting further. Alexander II, the new Czar of Russia, was convinced that peace must be made if only to give him an opportunity to re-organize his discredited armies, and the allies had no other target at which to aim. At last Napoleon felt that some of *la gloire* he yearned for was coming his way. Paris was chosen as the venue for the meetings that were to lead to the peace treaty, the Treaty of Paris, signed in March 1856. Here was

clear recognition of France's major standing in the eyes of the international community. Napoleon felt that he had now really made his mark and so did most of his contemporaries. The substance of the Treaty itself was of less significance than the appearance it gave of French importance. But one significant change had occurred in the pattern of international relationships: Russia had now joined France as a country against whom a punitive peace treaty had been made. Instead of a situation in which all the powers except France were in favour of maintaining the status quo, after 1856 the revisionists (those in Europe who wanted to change the state of affairs defined by international treaties), numbered two out of five. The effective isolation of France, which lay at the heart of her inferior status after 1815, had been well and truly broken.

In the years following the end of the Crimean War the Second Empire was at its height in international status and influence. This was in part because Napoleon III's image as a man of decisive and effective action was credible abroad, and in part because there was something of a vacuum in European politics, which the Emperor was able to fill. Since 1815 the hub of diplomatic affairs had been the Holy Alliance powers of Russia, Austria and Prussia, with Metternich orchestrating events from Vienna. The revolutions of 1848 had forced Metternich's resignation and there had been nobody to succeed him who would maintain the same degree of unity among the Eastern Powers. The Crimean War had soured relationships to a remarkable degree, especially as Austria had not only failed to support Russia but had also seemed to take advantage of her difficulties to strengthen her own position at the mouth of the River Danube. The resentment caused by this action had been considerable and had left Russia and Austria barely on speaking terms.

Napoleon III was quick to exploit this situation. Now that a peace treaty had been signed he could see no reason for continued animosity between Russia and France, a view that was shared by Alexander II. So began a short period of Franco–Russian friendship, boosted by French loans, that was to reinforce the feeling that France was once more the leading Power in Europe. French advice was listened to and French influence was exerted in all parts of Europe. Even as far away as the mouth of the Danube, it was French influence that led to the unification of the principalities of Moldavia and Wallachia to form the new state of Romania between 1859 and 1861. This was achieved despite the initial opposition of Russia, Austria and Turkey, the three countries most affected by the changes.

In the late 1850s Napoleon III was full of ambitious plans that would have turned the balance of power in Europe upside down and would have totally destroyed the pattern set up at Vienna in 1815. It is a sign of France's prestige that all the other major powers took the suggestions fairly seriously and expended considerable diplomatic energy in attempting to ensure that the plans came to nothing. It is no wonder that Napoleon III thought he was now the most powerful statesman in

Europe and believed there was no clear limit to what could be achieved.

b) Napoleon III and Italy

The first of the major plans that came to fruition concerned the future of Italy. A mixture of motives led Napoleon to want 'to do something for Italy'. His notion of supporting nationalities inclined him in this direction, as did the emotional attachment he felt to the country. In 1830, as a young man, he had been involved in a revolutionary attempt to overthrow the existing regimes in the northern states so that a united Italy could be formed. Although the exact nature of his contribution to the cause at this stage is uncertain, it is clear that he regarded himself as being committed to do what he could to help Italian nationalists achieve their ends. He also realized that any change to the status quo in Italy would seriously undermine the Vienna Settlement, thus making it likely that there would be further changes elsewhere. Once again, it seemed that he had something to gain and nothing to lose by fomenting disturbances abroad.

Throughout his period of power Napoleon III was better at dreaming about possibilities than at taking decisive action. It therefore seems likely that little would have happened very speedily had his hand not been forced. In January 1858 an Italian nationalist, Count Orsini, attempted to assassinate him. In a much publicized trial Orsini emphasized the fact that he had only framed his plot because Napoleon had failed to do what he had promised to help Italy. Although Orsini was guillotined in order to pacify those who demanded that the law be upheld, Napoleon was deeply moved by what had happened and was spurred on to action. In this he was helped by the existence of a politician in the Kingdom of Piedmont who was able to take charge of events and move them in the direction he wanted. Count Cavour had been Prime Minister in Piedmont since 1852 and was a skilled manipulator. He was more than a match for Napoleon III and was quickly able to seize the initiative once the Emperor had decided, in principle, to support the Italian nationalist cause. By 1858 it was clear that a peaceful solution to the problem could not be found. Austria was in control of most of Northern and Central Italy, either directly or through client rulers, and efforts to persuade her to exchange her Italian lands for territory elsewhere, perhaps in the Balkans, had fallen on deaf ears. To Napoleon III, as to Cavour, the only possibility seemed to be to drive out Austria by force of arms. The question was how and when this should be done, and what should take the place of Austrian rule once Northern Italy had been liberated.

* Cavour and Napoleon III met at Plombières in July 1858 to discuss tactics. Napoleon had in mind a limited military campaign to drive Austria from Lombardy and Venetia, the provinces she directly controlled. This was to be followed by the establishment of an Italian Confederation, probably under the Presidency of the Pope. In return for

French help, Piedmont would cede to France the areas of Savoy and Nice lying to the west of the Alps. Such an arrangement would be greatly to France's benefit. Austria would be weakened; a strand of the Vienna Settlement would be broken; a relatively weak neighbour, offering no threat to France, would be established; the Pope's temporal power would be increased to the satisfaction of the Church in France; and additional glory would come to Napoleon and to France. Cavour was prepared to accept this approach, knowing that once war had begun it would be possible to capitalize on events to bring about a situation that was more in Piedmont's interests. At Plombières his main purpose was to ensure that Napoleon's good intentions would be converted into direct action. This he succeeded in doing by extracting from Napoleon a promise that if Austria could be provoked into attacking Piedmont, France would intervene to free Italy from direct Austrian control.

* Plombières was followed by nine months of hectic diplomatic activity during which Austria was given every opportunity to withdraw gracefully. Napoleon seems genuninely to have hoped that war could be avoided, although the prospect of commanding French armies on the plains of northern Italy, as his uncle had done, thrilled him greatly. In the event the choice was not to be his. Cavour skilfully manoeuvred the angry and blustering Austrians into demanding a humiliating de-militarization in Piedmont. When this was refused war resulted in April 1859. France had no real option but to come to Piedmont's defence.

The war was fought with no great skill on either side. Two large scale battles took place, at Magenta and Solferino, both of which resulted in Austrian defeats, or at least tactical withdrawals. Lombardy was now free and the allies were on the point of moving into Venetia. Things were going well for Cavour and his rage and frustration can be imagined when he heard that Napoleon III had decided to proceed no further and had signed an armistice with Austria at Villafranca. By the terms of the armistice Austria was to give up Lombardy but to retain Venetia. The Austrian client states to the south of Lombardy and Venetia were to remain, and an Italian Confederation under the Pope was to be established.

The reasons for this about-turn by Napoleon have been argued over by historians. There is clearly no simple answer, but it is possible to identify the series of thoughts all of which led the Emperor towards the same conclusion. In emotional terms Napoleon was horrified by the terrible pain and suffering he witnessed on the battlefield of Solferino and he found he had little stomach for the realities of modern warfare. He wanted to avoid further battles if possible. At the same time he realized that so far only the easy part of the task had been undertaken. The Austrians were well entrenched in Venetia and huge casualties would have to be borne by any attacker who wished to dislodge them. Also there was some possibility that the Prussians would come to the aid of the Austrians, and Napoleon realized that his northern frontier was open to attack from the Prussians on the Rhine. To complete a dismal prospect, the war was reported to be unpopular in France where an early peace was hoped for. On the mental balance sheet that Napoleon drew up before making his decision the issue seemed clear. There were many good reasons for bringing the fighting to a close and no strong arguments in favour of continuing with the war. After all, France was getting almost all she had hoped for. The only exceptions were Austria's retention of Venetia and the fact that Piedmont would not now be bound to hand over Nice and Savoy. But the substance of victory was hers. An Italian Confederation, as a symbol of national aspirations, was to be formed; the terms of the Vienna Settlement were overturned; and France was once more seen to be shaping events by the force of her arms.

  * From the start of the Italian crisis Napoleon III had not really been in control of events; now he was reduced to being a virtually helpless spectator. Cavour had resigned in anger when he heard of Villafranca, but he was soon back in control in Piedmont, doing all he could to capitalize on events that were taking place in other parts of Italy. In the north Italian client states controlled by Austria popular uprisings were successful and were followed by demands for union with Piedmont, which Cavour persuaded France to allow. In Southern Italy, which neither Cavour nor Napoleon had any real wish to see incorporated in the enlarged Piedmont that was emerging, initial uprisings were turned into a popular crusade by Garibaldi and his 'thousand men'. The part played by Cavour in encouraging or facilitating Garibaldi's exploits is uncertain, but there is no doubt that Napoleon III could see that nothing but problems would result from successful revolutionary activity in Sicily and Naples. In the end, with Garibaldi threatening to push north to take Rome from the Pope, Napoleon was forced to agree to a Piedmontese army being allowed to invade the Papal States from the north in order to reach Garibaldi and bring his exploits to a halt. This was done and Garibaldi had the good grace to hand over his conquests to Victor Emmanuel, King of Piedmont. Thus what had started off for Napoleon III as an attempt to give limited help to Piedmont in driving Austria from Lombardy and Venetia, had resulted in the whole of Italy, except Venetia and Rome, being united under King Victor Emmanuel.

  * This was not greatly to Napoleon III's liking. It is true that now Piedmont had gained so much, France was able to extract Nice and Savoy as the price of support, but this hardly made up for the difficulties brought about by the creation of a large and secular Italian state. The plan to create a Confederation under the Pope had completely failed, and, what is worse, most of the Pope's existing territory had been taken over by the new Italy. All that was left was Rome, and this was only retained because of the presence of French troops. What started out as a venture designed to strengthen Napoleon III's position with the Catholics of France turned out to give them grave offence. Instead of being the man who had enhanced the power and prestige of the Papacy, Napoleon

III had become the supporter and enabler of those who sought to force the Pope to relinquish his temporal power as ruler of an independent state.

If this was not bad enough, France was now forced into the position of being a defender of the status quo, as far as Rome was concerned, in opposition to Italy which aspired to complete the process of unification begun in 1859 and 1860. Instead of having a Confederation of Italy as almost a client state, Napoleon III was faced with an Italy that, far from being grateful for what France had done to aid unification, was somewhat resentful that it was French troops that were preventing the acquisition of the historic capital.

* How far was Napoleon III to blame for what went wrong in his plans for Italy? His major mistake was to believe that he could retain control of the situation once war was declared. His decision not to honour the agreement made with Cavour at Plombières and to withdraw from the war before the Austrians had been driven out of Venetia failed to stabilize the situation and he then found himself without the moral authority to influence events significantly. His only hope of obtaining the outcome he desired would have been to combine with Austria in imposing, by force of arms if necessary, the terms of Villafranca on the reluctant Italians. But Napoleon was not the type of man to do this. He lacked both the ability to analyse the situation perceptively and the determination to pursue an unpopular course of action energetically. Instead of attempting to seize control of events, he allowed things to drift in the mistakenly optimistic belief that all would turn out well in the end. He failed to realize that he had little to gain and much to lose by letting events take their course. Yet it is only in retrospect that Napoleon's plans seem to have gone badly awry. At the time it appeared that France had been responsible for a successful attempt to overthrow the territorial arrangements made at Vienna in 1815. Napoleon III's international reputation stood higher than ever and it seemed that confirmation had been given of France's return to leading-power status. Certainly the Emperor himself imagined that France was now the dominant Power in Europe, and that further triumphs of foreign policy lay ahead.

3 Decline and Failure

For the remainder of Napoleon III's reign there were several major diplomatic initiatives underway at any one time. Some rapidly came to nothing; others were persevered with for some time before being abandoned. Some resulted in minor successes, but mostly there was failure. The victories of the 1850s were not to be repeated in the 1860s.

The reasons for this change of fortune are not difficult to identify. To some extent Napoleon was unfortunate in that chance factors worked against him and in Bismarck, at least, he found himself up against an adversary who was one of the century's experts in diplomacy. But much of Napoleon's misfortune resulted from his own way of doing things. He seemed to approach foreign affairs in much the same way as a professional gambler approaches card games. He believed that he was born lucky and that if he kept trying he would run into a lucky streak. This false confidence was often a substitute for careful thought and stopped him recognizing when he was in fact holding a losing hand. Whereas, at first, his air of certainty had done much to convince people that he was, an effective statesman, as time went on it was more and more widely recognized that he was largely bluff. Coupled with seriously declining health which made it difficult to concentrate on anything for long, Napoleon III's approach to foreign affairs made it likely that there would be fewer successes than failures.

a) Napoleon III and Mexico

A typical example of this is the Mexican Affair, which Napoleon slipped into almost by chance. Once he was involved, he became more and more committed and was almost the last person to see that he had a disaster on his hands from which he should disentangle himself at the earliest opportunity. It was this affair more than anything which caused people to question Napoleon's judgement and grasp of foreign affairs. His reputation never recovered from the disgrace of such a dramatic failure.

Mexico had been part of the Spanish Empire which had included most of South and Central America and much of the south and west of North America. During and immediately following the Napoleonic Wars all Spain's mainland American colonies had broken free and declared their independence as republics, aided and abetted by Great Britain. Mexico, in common with many of the other republics, was politically unstable and rapidly earned a reputation for inefficient and corrupt government as head of state followed head of state in rapid succession. Most changes of government were accompanied by revolutions during which there was a traditional round of rape, murder and the confiscation of property. Between 1821 and 1861 the average government lasted for less than a year. Strangely enough in these circumstances, many Mexican governments found it relatively easy to raise loans on the European money markets, especially London and Paris, and soon the situation was reached in which money was being borrowed in order to pay off previous loans. This was a worrying situation for European investors, especially small private banks, but was no different from the state of affairs in a dozen other countries.

Similarly worrying, although by no means exceptional, were the complaints of recent European settlers, largely from Spain, France and Britain, who as foreigners were exploited, often viciously, by whichever group happened to be in power at the time. There were constant pleas for armed intervention in order to restore political and financial stability, but these were ignored as a matter of routine by the European governments involved. It was almost as if governments felt that people who were silly enough to go to live there or to lend money to the country got what they deserved.

However, by 1861, there came together a chance grouping of factors that led to a reversal of earlier policies. In Mexico itself there was the return to power in January 1861 of Benito Juarez who had the distinction of being one of the few social revolutionaries to gain power in the country in the nineteenth century. He was not a part of the aristorcratic merry-go-round by which government succeeded government but with a conti-nuing policy of protecting the rich and exploiting the poor. Juarez wished to destroy the rich and to do something to improve the lot of the poor, although his main motivation seems to have been to gain riches and power for himself. In keeping with this approach, he confiscated the land of the Church and attempted to destroy its organization. He also decided to suspend the repayment of the Government's debt for two years. To the aristocratic governments of Europe here seemed to be a new type of monster worthy of special consideration.

Although the United States of America had played little part in international affairs since it had gained independence in the 1780s, it had generally managed to enforce a policy of preventing intervention by European Powers in the affairs of the American continents. But in 1861 the USA was in no position to act in the matter for she was fully occupied by her own Civil War. Had it not been for this, European states would not have seriously contemplated intervention in Mexico.

* For many years expatriate Mexicans in France had been attempting to gain support for the idea of supplying Mexico with a monarch from one of the leading European royal families. Few people had taken them seriously until the Empress Eugénie began to favour their case. As a fervent Catholic she was apparently impressed by the need to overthrow Juarez with his virulent anti-Clericalism, and replace him with a mon-arch who would protect the interests of the Church. Historians cannot agree about the extent to which Eugénie influenced Napoleon over this, but at the very least it was one more factor in favour of action being taken.

Napoleon III had for years seen Mexico as one of the strategically important parts of the world. Its significance was that it contained the natural land-crossing between the Atlantic and Pacific Oceans and as such should have a great future as a staging post in a large amount of world trade. Napoleon's dream was of a Mexico, probably enlarged to include all of Central America, dominated by France and acting as a counter-balance to the Anglo-Saxon states to the north. The dream suddenly seemed realizable with the United States apparently in the process of disintegration. But even now nothing would have happened had the British government been hostile. Fortunately for France there was a change of policy in London and Napoleon's approaches over joint intervention met a positive response.

There were many initiatives that Napoleon III could have taken in

1861. Because of chance factors Mexico turned out to be the major one and the Emperor was prepared to follow where fate appeared to lead. Once again, there seemed to be many possible advantages in intervening and few, if any, potential drawbacks.

* In October 1861 France, Britain and Spain agreed on a joint intervention in Mexico. From the outset there was every likelihood of misunderstandings because the partners were less than frank with one another. Napoleon especially was devious in the extreme, and Britain and Spain did not realize that he was seriously intending to re-establish a monarchy in Mexico by force of arms. They believed that they were engaged in a small-scale punitive expedition designed to persuade Jaurez that it was unwise to suspend debt payments. They therefore withdrew once this had been done. France stayed because by now Napoleon had become captivated by the possibilities that existed. After all, it was well known that Mexico was largely unable to defend herself. In 1848 the USA had attacked her and secured possession of 60 per cent of her territory, – the present states of Texas, New Mexico, California, Arizona and Utah. All the advice given to Napoleon indicated that a few thousand men would be able to make short work of the Mexican army. What is more, a suitable and willing candidate had been found for the Mexican throne. This was no less a person than Maximillian, the brother of the Austrian Emperor. It is little wonder that Napoleon thought that he was approaching his finest hour.

However, it was not to be. The Mexican army was dealt with comparatively swiftly as a formal fighting force, but Juarez and his supporters then resorted to a brand of guerrilla fighting that was virtually impossible to combat even though France eventually had 40 000 seasoned troops operating against them. To anybody with an open mind it was obvious by 1864 that a victory could not be won. The irregular troops of Juarez, hidden and fed by the Mexican people who hated foreigners even more than they detested the banditry of their own soldiers, were able to pick off small units of the occupying forces almost at will. Yet it was in 1864 that the Archduke Maximilian was taken to Mexico and installed as Emperor, at a time when even he doubted whether his mission was possible. For three years the struggle was maintained before Napoleon III finally admitted that he could not win and withdrew his troops. A few months later, in June 1867, Maximilian was captured by Juarez' men. He was executed by firing squad.

* It would be possible to be too hard on Napoleon III over the Mexican Affair. All the advice that Napoleon had received had confirmed the common-sense assumption that the people of Mexico would do little to support the forces of a brutal and tyrannical government, even if the suggestions by the supporters of the Catholic Church in Mexico that the people would rise up to welcome the liberators had owed more to optimism than to hard fact.

What is less excusable in the leader of a major Power is the way in which Napoleon was blinded to the reality of the situation by an increasingly romantic dream. This involved the creation of a Mexican Empire to lead a revival of Latin (as opposed to Anglo-Saxon) civilization in Central America and to become a major economic force in the region capable of counter-balancing the states of North America. Because he passionately wished this to be the case, he believed that it would be so, even when most of those around him could see that a realistic hope no longer existed. Napoleon's irresponsibility and refusal to face reality was highlighted in the minds of contemporaries by the tragic and dramatic end to Maximilian's reign, which followed the spectacle of his wife, driven mad by her experiences in Mexico, unsuccessfully touring the courts of Europe pleading support for her husband before it was too late. The Mexican Affair is the best example of Napoleon's power of self-delusion and of his ability to confuse a dream with reality and appearance with substance.

b) Napoleon III and Europe

While the Mexican fiasco had been slowly unfolding, the situation in Europe had been developing in a way that was not to Napoleon III's liking. After the bloodshed of the war in northern Italy in 1859 it was clearly the will of the people that France should not be involved again in a major European conflict. This view was supported by the Emperor, who hoped that he had done enough to establish France's military reputation and that he would be able to play the role of arbiter in European affairs without recourse to further military action. But as the years passed, it became obvious that this was not to be, for the major powers were not prepared to follow France's lead unless it was backed by the use of military might. It was as if the stakes had been raised in a card game played for money, with Napoleon unwilling to wager at the higher level. Bismarck, in particular, was not prepared to allow France any advantage unless she was willing to fight for it. Thus Napoleon found himself left more and more on the diplomatic sidelines, until a situation was reached where France had either to fight or to accept that she was no longer the major Power she wished to be. When, in 1870, the decision was made to fight, the disastrous outcome of the war resulted directly in the collapse of the Second Empire.

The nature of the new state of affairs was, of course, only slowly appreciated by people at the time, for changes in people's perception of a country's international standing usually lag some way behind reality. Perhaps a few diplomats realized in the early 1860s that Napoleon's France was not as strong as it appeared to be, but Napoleon III himself only came to recognize it latterly, and then refused to accept it, while the population of France cried out for war in 1870 unaware that events had overtaken them. Yet, for those who cared to recognize them, all the signs were there in the series of diplomatic reverses from 1863 onwards.

* In the Treaty of Vienna in 1815 the land that had been Poland in the

eighteenth century was divided between Russia, Austria and Prussia. The Poles had traditionally looked to France to lend them support in their struggles with avaricious neighbours, but in 1815 France was in no position to offer assistance. As it was not until 1918 that an independent Poland was again established, the 'Polish Question' remained a live issue in France throughout the nineteenth century, kept on the boil by the large number of Polish *émigrés* who resided in Paris.

Napoleon felt a similar emotional commitment to the Poles that he felt towards the Italians and it was widely expected that he would do something to help them when the time was right. That time appeared to have come in 1863 when a major uprising took place in Russian Poland and the Tsar's forces were thrown very much onto the defensive. If Napoleon had been more of a realist, able to recognize the difference between the desirable and the possible, he might have handled the situation more effectively. As it was he failed to think through the implications of his actions, tending to react to the pressures of the moment, buoyed up by the belief that it would all work out well in the end.

Urged on by public opinion in France, he protested to the Russians in the strongest possible terms about the severity with which the uprising was being suppressed and let it be known that he would not stand idly by while the rights of the Poles to nationhood were being trampled underfoot. When little more than polite notice was taken of his blusterings he was impotent to do more. So the mass of diplomatic activity did the Poles no good at all, while deep offence was given to the Russians who now regarded the close relationship that had existed between Russia and France since 1856 as being at an end. Thus a good friend had been lost and nothing had been gained. This situation could have been foreseen from the outset. It was clear that Russia had too much at stake to give way, except under the most direct pressure. In any case none of the other Powers would have tolerated the passage of French armies across Germany to reach the scene of the fighting even had Napoleon and the people of France wanted it, which they did not. Napoleon III would have done better to make sufficient of a protest to satisfy moderate public opinion, while assuring Alexander II of his continued friendship. Instead, he allowed himself to be ruled by his dream of a Europe made up of nation states and his emotional commitment to Poland's cause.

* If Napoleon III seems to have learned nothing from the experience, Bismarck, observing from Prussia, did. He could now be fairly sure that whatever action was taken against French interests, short of inflicting a major humiliation on her, there would be little action to back up the torrent of protest that was sure to be forthcoming. So, as Bismarck calculated the moves necessary to establish Prussian dominance in Germany, he could rightly discount the need to buy French acceptance of the changes he intended.

Thus in 1864 when Austria and Prussia joined forces to fight

Denmark, French protests led to nothing. Similarly in 1866 when Bismarck challenged Austria and by defeating her gained control of the whole of northern Germany, French inactivity was assured by vague promises of the possibility of territorial compensation on the left bank of the Rhine. In particular, Bismarck dangled before Napoleon the prospect of France acquiring Luxemburg. Those possibilities were, of course, abandoned by Prussia once the emergency was over and peace had been made with Austria. Napoleon III was left feeling cheated, in that French neutrality had been bought by Prussia for nothing, but it was too late to do anything about it. In fairness, though, it should be pointed out that most of the diplomats and statesmen of Europe were guilty of misreading the situation and assuming that there would be no swift victory for Prussia in a war with Austria. It was only once it had happened that it seemed obvious to so many people.

c) The Franco–Prussian War

So in the major international dealings of the 1860s France was almost as ineffectual as she had been at times under Louis–Philippe. Napoleon III was outmanoeuvred at every turn and by 1868 his standing was at a low ebb, just at the time when a sure hand was needed to handle a most complex situation in Spain and Portugal that was coming to a head. Both the states in the Iberian Peninsula had, for many years, suffered political instability, often culminating in outbreaks of civil war. Of the major Powers, only Britain and France had played a significant part in the political intrigue that had become a permanent feature of life in Spain and Portugal, and which mainly had to do with planning who should occupy the thrones of the two countries in the future. Britain had for two centuries regarded Portugal as a client state and had freely intervened in its domestic affairs in order to ensure that a friendly government was in power, and that Britain's dominant position in trade with Portugal and her colonies was maintained. France, on the other hand, looked upon Spain as her particular preserve and expected to have a major say in what happened there.

Both Britain and France recognized that by working together they were more likely to achieve what they wanted than if they chose to oppose one another. So Napoleon III tried to work in concert with Britain whenever possible. This was not always easy, for both sides suspected that the other would take an unfair advantage if she could. In particular, the British were suspicious of the French, especially when Napoleon III floated the idea of working towards a union of Spain and Portugal, with France possibly gaining some territorial compensation from Spain. This seemingly unrealistic flight of fancy became a practical possibility in 1868 when the crown of Spain was declared vacant and when the most likely successor appeared to be the King of Portugal. Britain was determined to stop this happening, while Napoleon III could not resist the temptation of attempting to gain an advantage for France. Lengthy negotiations took place, with France hoping to obtain British consent to a proposal that would lead to the unification of Spain and Portugal. As the months passed and a solution to the problem seemed no nearer, the leading figures in Spanish political life grew impatient and were tempted to seek their own solution to a problem which France and Britain appeared unable to resolve.

Bismarck, in Prussia, was not slow to see that here was a situation from which he might be able to secure some diplomatic advantage. Prussia had played little part in Spanish affairs previously, but now the claims of Leopold of Hohenzollern (a member of the Prussian royal family, although not a close relation of the King) to the crown of Spain were pressed energetically. If Britain and France had reached an agreement reasonably speedily little would have been heard of this. As they did not, and as the leading Spanish politicians were looking for a candidate of their own as Britain and France seemed incapable of supplying them with one, the 'Hohenzollern Candidature' became a major issue. At first it looked as if Bismarck had overstepped the mark and would be forced to back-off, with a consequent loss of face. In June 1870 Leopold was offered the crown of Spain and Bismarck ensured that the offer was accepted. This was an untenable position if Napoleon III showed any resolve at all. Prussia had as little chance of imposing her will in Spain against the wishes of France, as France had of achieving an outcome in Poland that was contrary to the interests of Russia. In both cases the Power seeking to influence events was geographically remote while the country that had something to lose was close at hand.

* The reaction in France to the news that Leopold of Hohenzollern had accepted the throne of Spain was predictable. Public opinion was outraged at this action which seemed especially calculated to show the world that Prussia was now more influential than France in European affairs. It was viewed as a serious challenge and a clear insult that must be rebuffed in the strongest terms possible. The newspapers demanded war, the politicians demanded war, and even Napoleon III himself, who was now so ill that he took little part in day-to-day politics, was prepared to accept that if Prussia did not retract war must come. The King of Prussia could see that his minister had gone too far and that there was no alternative to giving way. The acceptance was withdrawn and to Napoleon III, at least, it appeared that the crisis was over.

But the people of France were not so easily satisfied. There were widespread demands that action be taken to avenge the way in which France had been insulted. A suggestion was made that the King of Prussia should be asked to guarantee that the candidature of Leopold would never be put forward again. This idea was seized upon by the Empress Eugénie and the court circle and the Emperor was prevailed upon to support it. The request was made by the French Ambassador in Berlin, but it was politely refused on the basis that it was just as insulting to Prussia as had been the original acceptance of the crown to France. It was at this stage that Bismarck, in the famous 'Ems Telegram', amended the report of the King of Prussia's refusal to give the guarantees sought, in such a way that it looked as if France had been insulted once again. War fever once again ran high in France, and this time there seemed no way of gaining a diplomatic triumph that would avert to resort to arms. With cries of '*À Berlin*', war was declared on Prussia on 19 July 1870.

  * From the French point of view, what followed was a complete disaster. The French armies mobilized more slowly than the Prussian, and rather than marching on Berlin, Napoleon III and his commanders found themselves defending their own territory. It is perhaps symtomatic of the French overconfidence that their troops were issued with maps of Germany, but not of their own country. As defeat followed defeat it became clear that a huge miscalculation had been made. On 1 September 1870, only six weeks after the declaration of war, Napoleon III was forced to surrender with 84 000 men when they were surrounded and hopelessly outgunned at Sedan in northern France. The war went on, but with the Emperor a prisoner of the enemy and the Empress and her son fleeing to England, the Second Empire came to a sudden end. A Republic was declared, not so much in anger but in order to fill a void that had been left unexpectedly. The regime had not been overthrown; it had collapsed.

  The lead-up to the Franco–Prussian war of 1870 was in many ways a typical example of the way in which Napoleon III conducted foreign affairs, although his personal responsibility for what happened is less direct than in earlier years. Stances were taken up without careful thought being given to the likely consequences; there was an unrealistic confidence that all would turn out well in the end; and, although Napoleon III had accurate knowledge about the reality of the situation, the relative military strengths of France and Prussia was assessed on the basis of wishful thinking rather than hard fact.

  The outcome of the war itself was really a case of Napoleon III paying the price for his actions. By the clumsy ways in which he had attempted to promote French interests in foreign affairs he had made all the other powers suspicious of him. By the particular polices he had adopted he had turned all his potential friends into potential enemies. Russia, Austria, Britain and Italy were all sympathetic to Prussia in the war, especially when Bismarck was able to release documents showing that for years France had been attempting to gain territory on the left bank of the Rhine, an area of possible French aggrandisement that the other powers had often co-operated to defend. Many people throughout Europe thought that Napoleon III was merely getting what he deserved.

4 Napoleon III and the Second Empire: Conclusion

Napoleon III's defeat in the Franco–Prussian War led to the fall of his regime and to his exile in England where he died in 1873. Most of those who have written about the Second Empire, its achievements and significance, have been less than flattering. This is especially so of contemporary authors who were moved to write largely because they were hostile to the regime. Victor Hugo was one of the first to appear in print. His attack on the man who had broken his oath to uphold the constitution of the Second Republic when he carried out the *coup d'état* of 2 December 1851, and who had compounded his crime by massacring hundreds of innocent Parisians in the days that followed, appeared in the summer of 1852. The title of his book was *Napoleon the Little*. He was in no doubt as to how historians would view the nephew of the great Emperor.

1   It may, perhaps, be flattering to the self-love of M. Bonaparte to be caught hold of by history at all; but if he chance to have, and truly one would imagine so, any illusion in his head as to his value as a political miscreant, let him divest himself of it.
5   Let him not imagine, because he had piled up horror on horror, that he will ever hoist himself up to the elevation of the great historical bandits. We have been, perhaps, wrong, in some pages of this book, here and there, in mentioning his name at all, in connection with theirs. Though he has committed enormous crimes, he
10 will remain paltry. He will never be other than the nocturnal strangler of liberty; he will never be other than the man who has intoxicated his soldiers, not with glory, like the first Napoleon, but with wine; he will never be other than the pigmy tyrant of a great people. Grandeur, even in infamy, is utterly inconsistent with the
15 character and calibre of the man. As Dictator, he is a buffoon; let him make himself Emperor, he would be grotesque. That would at once put an end to him. His destiny is to make mankind shrug their shoulders.

Like many commentators at the time and since, Hugo offered a simple explanation of Louis Napoleon and his motivation.

1   Before the 2nd December, the leaders of the Right used habitually to say of Louis Bonaparte; *'tis an idiot.* They were mistaken. Questionless, that brain of his is perturbed, and has large gaps in it, but you can discern here and there in it, thoughts consecutive and
5   concatenate. 'Tis a book whence pages have been torn. Louis Napoleon has a fixed idea; but a fixed idea is not idiotcy; he knows what he wants, and he goes straight on to it through justice, through law, through reason, through honesty, through humanity, no doubt, but, still, straight on.
10   He is not an idiot. He is a man of another age than our own. He seems absurd and mad, because he is out of his place and time. Transport him in the 16th century to Spain, and Philip II. would

recognise him; to England, and Henry VIII. would smile on him; to Italy, and Cæsar Borgia would embrace him.

15   The only thing is that he forgets, or knows not, that in the age wherein we live, his actions will have to traverse the grand courses of human morality, chastened by three ages of literature and by the French revolution; and that, in this medium, his actions will wear their true aspect, and appear what they really are – hideous.

20   His partisans – he has some – complaisantly parallel him with his uncle, the first Bonaparte They say: "The one accomplished the 18th Brumaire, the other the 2nd December: they are two men of ambition." The first Bonaparte aimed to reconstruct the empire of the West; to make Europe his vassal; to dominate over the con-
25   tinent by his power, and to dazzle it by his grandeur; to take an arm-chair himself, and give footstools to the kings; to create his place in history: Nimrod, Cyrus, Alexander, Hannibal, Cæsar, Charlemagne, Napoleon: to be master of the world. He was so. To be so, he accomplished the 18th Brumaire. The other man aims to
30   have horses and women, to be called *Monseigneur*, and to live luxuriously. To this end, he brought about the 2nd December. Yes: they are two men of ambition: the comparison is just.

Let us add, that, like the first Bonaparte, the second also aims to be Emperor. But that which somewhat allays comparisons is, that
35   there is, perhaps, a slight difference between conquering an empire and pilfering it.

Napoleon III would have agreed with Hugo that he had a strong sense of purpose but would have disagreed with the definition of it. As far as he was concerned, in words spoken within days of the establishment of the Second Empire, his aim was 'to found a stable government which has for its basis religion, honest dealing, justice and the love of the suffering classes.'

But few would agree that this is what actually happened, even if they would equally reject Marx's analysis written within a few months of the Second Empire's destruction.

1   The Empire, with the *coup d'état* for its certificate of birth, universal suffrage for its sanction, and the sword for its sceptre, professed to rest upon the peasantry, the large mass of producers not directly involved in the struggle of capital and labour. It
5   professed to save the working class by breaking down Parliamentarism, and, with it, the undisguised subserviency of Government to the propertied classes. It professed to save the propertied classes by upholding their economic supremacy over the working class; and, finally, it professed to unite all classes by reviving for all the
10   chimera of national glory. In reality, it was the only form of government possible at a time when the bourgeoisie had already

lost, and the working class had not yet acquired the faculty of
ruling the nation. It was acclaimed throughout the world as the
saviour of society. Under its sway, bourgeois society, freed from
15 political cares, attained a development unexpected even by itself.
Its industry and commerce expanded to colossal dimensions; financial swindling celebrated cosmopolitan orgies; the misery of the
masses was set off by a shameless display of gorgeous, meretri-
cious, and debased luxury. The State power, apparently soaring
20 high above society and the very hotbed of all its corruptions. Its
own rottenness, and the rottenness of the society it had saved, were
laid bare by the bayonet of Prussia, herself eagerly bent upon
transferring the supreme seat of that *régime* from Paris to Berlin.

As with most significant issues in history, a simple explanation can
never do justice to the complexities of Napoleon III and the Second
Empire. He was not a man of coherent views or consistent action, nor was
his regime blessed with any unity of purpose. No one pattern will fit the
events that took place in France between 1852 and 1870. This point was
well made by Theodore Zeldin in the conclusions he reached in 1973
about Napoleon III.

1 The usual view is that he was a well-meaning visionary out of touch
   with reality, a confused charlatan, a feeble parody of his uncle, an
   adventurer whose bluff and gambles were doomed to a catastrophic
   end. He owes this reputation partly to the repeated fiascos of his
5 foreign policy and partly to the fact that the majority of intellectuals
   of his day were opposed to his regime; he has never quite recovered
   from their witty and pungent attacks. In the twentieth century,
   there has been, almost inevitably, a reaction to this hostile interpretation. Some historians have instead painted him, not as aping the
10 past, but as a man far ahead of his time, principally concerned with
   the economic development of his country, a precursor of techno-
   cracy and of the modern dictators. This is to go too far in the
   opposite direction. For Napoleon III cannot be classified accurately in any single category. One should not assume that he was a
15 man with certain set ideas, which he described in his books and
   which he then put into practice when he became emperor.

What must be accepted is that any judgment of the Emperor and his
Empire which relies on sweeping generalizations is unsatisfactory. There
is no way in which the reality of the political life of France under
Napoleon III can be encapsulated in a few sentences. What can be done,
however, is that each student who writes about the subject can draw
attention to the lack of a simple pattern and can illustrate those trends
and tendencies which seem most pertinent to the line of enquiry being
followed. But the tentative nature of conclusions drawn and judgments

made needs to be recognized with Napoleon III, and more so than with many historical characters. He worked hard to hide his true feelings and intentions from friend and enemy alike. He wished to become and to remain a man of mystery. In this, at least, he was largely successful.

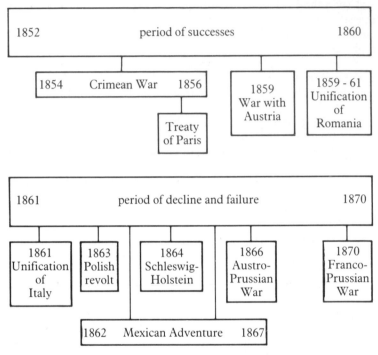

Summary – The Second Empire, 1852–70: Abroad

Making notes on *'The Second Empire, 1852–70: Abroad'*

When you are making notes on 'The Second Empire: Abroad', remember throughout that your aim is to gain an understanding of Napoleon III's foreign policy: what he did, why he did it, and what were the consequences. You will read about some highly important international affairs – such as the Crimean War, the unification of Italy and Germany, and the Polish question – all of which are worthy of study in their own right. In this context, however, you only need to know about them in so far as they affected or reflected French foreign policy. You are likely to make full notes on these events when studying topics other than France, 1814–70. So do not make notes that do not aid your current concern to understand international affairs from France's point of view.

The following headings and sub-headings should prove helpful:

1.   The approach to foreign affairs
1.1. *'l'Empire c'est la paix'*
1.2. Destruction of the Vienna Settlement
1.3. Nationalism
1.4. *La gloire*
1.5. Territorial expansion
1.6. Satisfying public opinion
2.   Successes
2.1. The Crimean War
      Causes
      Course
      Consequences
2.2. Napoleon III and Italy
      Motives
      The plan
      War with Austria
      Italian Unification
      Consequences
      Conclusions
3.   Decline and Failure
3.1. Reasons
3.2. Napoleon III and Mexico
      Background
      Motives
      Events
      Conclusion
3.3. Napoleon III and Europe
      The changed situation
      Poland
      Bismarck
3.4. The Franco–Prussian War
      Background in Spain
      Immediate causes
      Events
4.   Napoleon III and the Second Empire: Conclusion

Answering essay questions on *'The Second Empire, 1852–70'*

It is probable that at some stage you will be expected to use evidence from the previous two chapters in answering general questions on the period 1814–70. There is a discussion of these questions on pages 130–131.

But more frequently you will be asked to answer questions that relate exclusively to the Second Empire. Such questions tend to concentrate on

four aspects of the period:
1. changes in the political system;
2. economic and social developments;
3. foreign affairs;
4. the role of Napoleon III.

Although the first three aspects could be written about in isolation, you will rarely be asked to do this. Normally you will be required to handle several aspects in one essay, especially as the role of Napoleon III can only be understood by reference to the other three aspects. It is therefore essential that you acquire a knowledge and understanding of *all* the issues discussed in the previous two chapters.

Study carefully the following questions:

1. 'What were Napoleon III's strengths and weaknesses as a statesman?' (Oxford and Cambridge, 1983)

2. 'How effectively did Napoleon III solve the problems which had brought about the fall of the July Monarchy?' (WJEC, 1981)

3. ' "A desperate remedy for a desperate condition." How fair is this comment on Napoleon III's liberalisation of his Empire?' (Cambridge, 1981)

4. 'How successful were the social and economic policies of Napoleon III?' (Cambridge, 1981)

5. ' "He promised much, he achieved little." Do you regard this as a suitable epitaph for Napoleon III?' (Scottish, 1981)

6. ' "It was the policies of Napoleon III rather than those of Bismarck which led to the Franco–Prussian War of 1870." Discuss this statement.' (JMB, 1981)

7. 'With what justification may it be argued that the Second French Empire deserved its fate?' (AEB, 1982)

8. 'To what extent did France benefit from the domestic policies of the Second Empire?' (London, 1978)

9. ' "Despite the short life of the Second French Republic, republicanism retained considerable influence under Napoleon III." Discuss.' (Oxford, 1980)

10. 'How successful was Napoleon III in keeping his promise that his Empire would mean economic progress?' (JMB, 1979)

11. 'To what extent was Napoleon III a liberal?' (Oxford and Cambridge, 1979)

12. ' "Napoleon III's domestic policies bestowed great boons on the French people, yet his regime collapsed because to so many people Bonapartism stood not for peace, but for military glory." Discuss.' (SUJB, 1979)

13. 'How stable was Napoleon III's Empire, at home and abroad?' (Oxford and Cambridge, 1980)

For each question, note down which of the four aspects would need to be included in an answer. Indicate where it would be necessary to consider issues not discussed in the previous two chapters. From your list you should be able to see how important it is to acquire an understanding of all the issues discussed in the previous two chapters.

With the exception of the first question, all the questions are either of the 'How far/to what extent?' or the 'challenging statement' type. Check that this is so. Thus only for the first question would an answer made up of a number of general points, each backed up with evidence, be appropriate. For all the other questions it is essential that you 'argue a case' in your answers.

General approaches which between them would suit all the questions are:

a)   In the following ways/to the following extent *Yes*, (up to three paragraphs, each on a topic or an aspect of a topic where *Yes* applies); in the following ways/to the following extent *No*, (up to three paragraphs, each on a topic or an aspect of a topic where *No* applies).

b)   as a), but with the two halves of the essay reversed.

What criteria would you use in deciding whether to adopt general approach a) or general approach b)? Would they have to do with the relative strength of the two sides of the argument?

Look at question 7. Make two lists. In one, include the points that would support the arguments, 'Yes, the Second French Empire deserved its fate.' In the other, include the points that you could use on the *No* side of the argument. When you have listed all the points you can think of, form them into groups so that you have two or three general points on each side of the argument. There are several possible groupings that could work equally well, so there is no single correct answer. *But* it is unlikely that your groupings are appropriate unless they allow you to include central issues such as 'the wish to win glory in foreign affairs without a willingness to pay the price', 'the ability of the political system to change in order to retain majority support', 'the relative lack of attention paid to the needs of the poor', and 'the development of Paris into the diplomatic, cultural and leisure capital of Europe'.

In what order would you present the two sides to the argument? Why?

Go through the same process with another question from the list above. You should finish up with up to six paragraph points (probably written as a phrase or a sentence) listed in the order in which you would write them. Add to this essay plan an indication of what would be the main point to be made in the introduction and in the conclusion.

Source-based questions on '*The Second Empire, 1852–70: Abroad*'

1 Victor Hugo's *Napoleon the Little*, 1852
Read carefully the two extracts from Victor Hugo's *Napoleon the Little* given on pages 123 and 124, and answer the following questions:

a) What internal evidence do the extracts contain as to their date of writing?
b) What method does Hugo use to attack Louis Napoleon?
c) What does Hugo claim were Louis Napoleon's motives in seeking power?
d) In what ways would these extracts be useful to a historian researching the political history of France in the 1850s?

2 The basis of the Second Empire

Read carefully Napoleon III's statement of his aim, given on page 124, and Marx's assessment of the Second Empire, given on pages 124–125. Answer the following questions:
a) Describe Marx's main complaint about the Second Empire.
b) Each extract lists four factors as the basis of the Second Empire. What area of overlap is there between the two lists
c) In what ways are the two statements about the aims of the Second Empire conceived in different terms?

Answering essay questions on 'France 1814–70'

As you will already have learned from the 'Answering essay questions' section at the end of the first chapter, (see pages 6–7), the major issue that has concerned historians about the whole period is France's relative political instability.

You should now be in a good position to think analytically about questions such as:

'Why was France unable to find a durable form of government between 1815 and 1871?' (London)

You will immediately recognize that questions like this are essentially about *causes*, and will remember the work you have already done on planning answers to questions about causation.

But you should notice a basic difference between the causation questions you have been considering earlier in the book and the question above. In earlier sections you have been thinking about the causes of *a particular event*, for example, the revolutions of 1830 and 1848. Now you are being asked to comment on *a continuing situation* – political instability lasting more than half a century.

The analytical tool of looking at long-term, short-term, and immediate causes, which works well when explaining why a particular event occurred and why a situation of limited duration existed, is less appropriate when considering continuing situations. More useful is an approach which distinguishes between the general and the specific. Thus it is possible to talk about *background causes* or *indirect causes* and about *particular causes* or *direct causes*.

When using this approach to answer a question on causation, it is usual to deal with background causes before particular causes – to move from the general to the specific.

The following phrases could all be used in describing the reasons for France's political instability between 1814 and 1870: the divisions between Left and Right; the economic slump of the late 1820s; the mistakes of Louis–Philippe; the legacy of the French Revolution; the unwillingness of the French to compromise; the Industrial Revolution; the tactics of Charles X; the political importance of Paris.

Divide the eight phrases into two groups: background causes and particular causes. Add phrases of your own to each group until you can think of no further causes of the political instability of the period. There is likely to be considerable overlap between the ideas represented by the phrases you have chosen. Scruntinize your list and eliminate as many areas of overlap as you can. If you are left with more than three phrases in each group you should look for phrases that are less specific. For example, in the list of eight phrases, above, it is possible to think of one phrase which would cover both points made in the third and seventh phrases, or both points made in the second and sixth phrases.

When you have reduced your list to at most six phrases, you will have chosen your major paragraph points. You may find it useful at this stage to follow through the procedure by deciding what supporting evidence you will include in each paragraph, identifying the main point to be made in the introduction and conclusion, and writing an answer to the question 'Why was France unable to find a durable form of government between 1815 and 1871?'

Further Reading

If you only have a short amount of time for further reading on this period of French history there is one book in particular that you should look at. This is:

Alfred Cobban, *A History of Modern France: volume 2: 1799–1945.* (Penguin)

Although it was first published in 1961, nothing to compare with it has subsequently been written in English. It is a little difficult in places and is best read once a basic understanding of the period has been gained, but it is full of memorable explanations and quotable phrases. Much is to be gained even if you read only a few of the 10–15 page sections into which the book is divided.

A second general history is also to be highly recommended. This is:

J.P.T. Bury, *France 1814–1940* (Methuen)

This first appeared in 1949 but it has been revised many times since. Although primarily aimed at university undergraduates, it is worth looking at if only to glance over the texts of the Charter of 1814 and the Constitutions of 1848 and 1852 which are printed in full (but in French).

Most of the general books on European history deal with France too briefly to be of much help to you once you have read this book. Two exceptions are:

The New Cambridge Modern History: volume IX, War and Peace in an age of upheaval, 1793–1830. (C.U.P., 1965)

which, despite its title, also deals with the reign of Louis–Philippe; and

J.A.S. Grenville, *Europe Reshaped, 1848–1878.* (Fontana, 1976)

which is particularly useful on the liberalizing of the Second Empire.

Biographies of the main characters of the period abound. Many of them are worth reading but you should not devote too much of your main study time to them. If you can treat them as 'bed-time' reading, to be picked up when you are not feeling up to 'proper' work, you will be using your time wisely. Even with this type of reading, always make notes. The publication details of the book (in case you wish to refer to it again) and a few sentences written after completing each chapter are usually sufficient with biographies.

Biographies written for the general reader are often the kind to be of interest to students at A-level. Two examples of such books with very readable texts and generally sound historical interpretation are:

T.E.B. Howarth, *Citizen-King* (Eyre and Spottiswoode, 1961) on Louis–Philippe; and,

W.H.C. Smith, *Napoleon III* (Wayland, 1972).

One biography writeen for the history student is old but well worth reading:

J.P.T. Bury, *Napoleon III and the Second Empire* (E.U.P., 1964).

Sources on France: Monarchy, Republic and Empire, 1814–70

There is no readily available collection of documentary source material covering the politics of this period in English translation. A collection that has some useful extracts relating to the Second Empire is:
1. **David Thomson**, *France: Empire and Republic, 1850–1940* (Macmillan 1968)
   But by far the richest sources of contemporary material are the memoirs and other writings of those living in France at the time. Many are not easily located but one is in general circulation and is well worth obtaining. It is:
2. **ed. J. P. Mayer**, *The Recollections of Alexis de Tocqueville* (Harvill Press, 1948)
   It contains first hand accounts of many of the events of 1848–50 as well as much comment.
   This can be backed up by extracts from volume one of:
3. **Marx and Engels**, *Selected Works* (Moscow, 1951)
   Some secondary works on the period contain short extracts from documentary sources. Two books that are particularly worth looking at for this and other reasons are:
4. **G. de Berthier de Sauvigny**, *The Bourbon Restoration*, translated by L. M. Case (University of Pennsylvania Press, 1966); and
5. **T. Zeldin**, *France 1848–1940* (OUP, 1973)
   A good range of illustrations on nineteenth-century European history is contained in:
6. **ed Asa Briggs**, *The Nineteenth Century* (Thames and Hudson), 1970

Acknowledgements

Acknowledgement is given for use of extracts as follows:
G. de Berthier de Sauvigny, *The Bourbon Restoration* Pages 22, 29, 30
T. E. B. Howarth, *Citizen King* (Eyre & Spottiswoods, 1961) pages 39, 40
ed. J. P. Mayer, *The Recollections of Alexis de Tocqueville* pages 40 (top), 57–8, 65, 67, 84–5
W. H. C. Smith, *Napoleon III* (Wayland, 1972) pages 73, 87, 93
David Thomson, *France: Empire and Republic, 1850–1914* pages 83–4
Marx and Engels, *Selected Works* pages 124–5
Victor Hugo, *Napoleon the Little* (Vizetelly & Co, 1852) pages 123–4
T. Zeldin, *France 1848–1940* page 125.

The author and Publishers wish to thank the following for their permission to use copyright illustrations:

Mansell Collection: cover (the coronation procession of Charles X to Rheims Cathedral, 1824), page 23.

The author and Publishers wish to thank the following examination boards for permission to include questions:
The Associated Examining Board; Joint Matriculation Board; Oxford and Cambridge Schools Examination Board; Southern Universities' Joint Board; University of Cambridge Local Examinations Syndicate; University of London School Examinations Department; University of Oxford Delegacy of Local Examinations; Welsh Joint Education Committee; Scottish Certificate of Education Examination Board. (The essay guidance sections are the responsibility of the General Editor and have not been approved by the Boards.)

Index